# AMERICAN
# BIG PICTURE

**B2** [UPPER INTERMEDIATE] Split Edition a

Student's Book / Workbook



SIMON BREWSTER ■ ALASTAIR LANE

Series editor: BEN GOLDSTEIN

Richmond

www.americanbigpicture.net

**Richmond**

58 St Aldates
Oxford
OX1 1ST
United Kingdom

Printed in Mexico

ISBN: **978-607-06-0759-2**

First edition: October 2012

Av. Río Mixcoac No. 274, Col. Acacias,
Del. Benito Juárez, C.P. 03240, México, D.F.

**Publisher:** Deborah Tricker
**Managing Editor:** Mary Todd
**Editors:** Eleanor Clements, Kate Chomacki
**Proofreader:** Anna Gunn

**Cover Design:** Pentacor Book Design
**Design & Layout:** Lorna Heaslip
**Picture Editors:** Magdalena Mayo and Helen Reilly/Arnos Design Ltd
**Art Coordinator:** Lorna Heaslip
**Illustrators:** Francis Blake c/o Three-in-a-Box Ltd., Roger Harris c/o NB Illustration, Sally Newton, Myles Talbot

**We would like to thank the following reviewers for their valuable feedback which has made *American Big Picture* possible. We extend our thanks to the many teachers and students not mentioned here.**

(Argentina): Cecilia Chiacchio, Ingrid Suhring; (Brazil): Ana Falcao, Virginia Garcia, Patricia McKay, Cynthia Phillipps, Bia Sousa; (Colombia): Kathleen Canal; (Italy): Morgan Cox, Karen Geiger, Sarah Stats; (Mexico): Emma Dominguez, Melissa Ferrin, Lupita Neve, Coral Ibarra Yunez; (Poland): Malgosia Adams, Marta Rosinska; (Spain): Vicki Anderson, Juan Carlos Araujo, Karen Dyer, Gabby Maguire, Fiona McClelland, Karin Rickatson, Almudena Verdugo Valcarce, Andy Walsh; (UK): Cathy Ellis, Howard Smith, Jonathan Stoddart

**Photos:**
Antiquities of the Prize Ring; Apple.com; Arnos Design Ltd; Jon Ayres; BBC; Bridgeman Art Library; China Photo Press; www.doggiefountain.com; Dyson; J. M.ª Escudero; Eyevine; Fairfax; Flickr/yeric; Ceri Jones; Kenwood; Masterfile; MEPL; Nigel's Eco Store; Nokia E7; S. Padura; Leslie Sturges; Scentsciences.com; Tengu; ThinkGeek.com; Vision Fine Art Gallery; Wales News Service; Wikipedia.

A. G. E. FOTOSTOCK; ALAMY/Imagebroker, Gary Roebuck, Spencer Grant, Ace Stock Ltd, Image Source, Netphoto, Digitallife, NetPics, David Bleeker Photography.com, Homer W Sykes, GOGO Images Agency, Robert Fried, Paul Ridsdale, Vario Images Gmbh & Co.KG, Apply Pictures, Keith Morris, The Photolibrary Wales, db images, PNC Photography, Melba Photo Agency, Galit Seligmann, Rubberball, AF Archive, MBI, allesaltag, Catchlight Visual Services, indiascapes, Greenshoots Communications, Agestock USA, Nigel Cattlin, Ragnar Sigurdsson, RIA Novosti, Pictorial Press, Moviestore Collection, Moreleaze Travel Spain, Thomas Cockrem, DW Images Scotland, David Crockett Photography, Julian Marshall, Stocksearch, Peter Widman, Alistair Scott, WoodyStock, James Caldwell, Andrea Magugliani, Francis Roberts, Larry Lilac, Squint, Patrick Eden, Peter Jordan, Paul Bradbury, Janine Wiedel, Foodfolio, Rafael Ben-Ari, Bill Bachmann, Alex Sagre, Yadid Levy; CORDON PRESS/ Corbis; CORBIS/Yi lu , Langevin/Sygma, Mika, Heide Benser, Gabe Palmer, The Food Passionates, Blend Images, Alan Copson, Bloimage, Kazushige Takashima, MM productions, Rachel Frank; DIGITALVISION; FOTOLIA/Photogersen, Ye Lien, Corepics, Suprijono Suharjoto; GETTY IMAGES/Steve Wisbauer, SNS Group, Adrian Weinbrecht, Arabian Eye Collection, Blend Images, John Lund/Marc Romanelli, Nancy Honey Collection, Ultra F Collection/Photodisc, Stone, Science Photo Library, Smith Collection, Comstock Collection, AFP, Amos Nachoum Barcroft USA, Samuel D. Barricklow Collection, Wireimage, NY Daily News, Islamic School, Mike Brinson Collection, Insy Shah, James L Stanfield/ National Geographic, Stefano Opo/Photodisc, Sue Flood, Dorota/ Bogdan Bialy, Carlos Davila, Michael Powell, AP, Digital Vision, Carl Court, Neil Emmerson, Lonely Planet Images, Paulo Fridman, Mark Serota, Stringer, Andrew Wong, DreamPictures, The Image Bank, Peter Dazeley, Peter Cade/Ionica, Jason Reed, Fuse, Image Source, Taxi, Jack Hollingsworth, Lu Beziat, Lifesize, Amana Images, Tom Craig, Amanda Voisard; GETTY IMAGES SALES SPAIN/Thinkstock, Photos.com Plus; ISTOCKPHOTO/Yury Kuzmin Lliangpv, Bjarki Reyr, Yes./Nuit, Wael Hamdan; ISTOCKPHOTO/Getty Images Sales Spain; MATTON-BILD; NATUREPL/Steven David Miller, Andrew Parkinson; PA PHOTOS/ Kimimasa Mayama, Joerg Carstensen, Peter Morrison, Kyoto News, Paul Sakuma; PHOTOS.COM/Elena Elisseeva, Jupiter Images, Milos Luzanin, David Simandl, Michelle Malven, Kevin Russ, Thinkstock, Comstock, Viktor Fischer, Dan Jordan, George Doyle, Claudiu Badea, Kai Chiang, Alexander Raths, Luoman, gioadventures, Pixland, Kenneth O Quinn, Stewart Cook, Fabian Brunsing, Keystone USA-ZUMA, Alex Segre, Ray Tang; SERIDEC PHOTOIMAGENES CD; THE PICTUREDESK/ Studio Canal, Warner Bros/Andrew Cooper; SHUTTERSTOCK/Corepics, Fotofactory; THINKSTOCK/Hemera, Istockphoto, Photodisc, Stockbyte, Getty Images, Digital Vision, Creatas; ARCHIVO SANTILLANA
© THINKSTOCK: Jupiterimages p. 94 (photos.com)

**Cover Photo:**
Big Apple at sunset, Fotolia © dell #9950038

The Publisher has made every effort to trace the owner of copyright material; however, the Publisher will correct any involuntary omission at the earliest opportunity.

This book was printed in los talleres de Editorial Impresora Apolo, S.A. de C. Centeno 150-6, Col. Granjas Esmeralda,C.P. 09810, México, D.F. in december 2012

# CONTENTS UNITS 1–6


| | Grammar | Vocabulary | Reading & Listening | Pronunciation |
|---|---|---|---|---|
| 1 **Social Networks** *page 4* | • Auxiliary Verbs<br>• Past Participles<br>• Reflexive Pronouns | • Relationships<br>• Phrasal verbs | (R) Broad Banned!<br>(L) A podcast about profile pictures<br>• Discussing family and friends | • Emphatic stress<br>• Intonation: question tags |

*page 12* **Functional Language:** small talk *page 13* **Speaking Task:** offering solutions
*page 152* **Writing Bank:** a question-and-answer post

| | Grammar | Vocabulary | Reading & Listening | Pronunciation |
|---|---|---|---|---|
| 2 **Experts** *page 14* | • The Present<br>• *Used to do/Used to doing* | • Health<br>• Medicine<br>• *...ever* | (R) Putting the Fun Back into Fitness<br>• We're All Experts Now<br>(L) Opinions about health issues<br>• An interview about a medical career | • Shifts in stress<br>• Intonation: stress |

*page 22* **Functional Language:** making polite requests *page 23* **Writing Task:** a blog post giving advice

| | Grammar | Vocabulary | Reading & Listening | Pronunciation |
|---|---|---|---|---|
| 3 **Survival** *page 24* | • Narrative Tenses<br>• Adverbs | • Survival<br>• Talking about danger<br>• Weather | (R) An article about the Chilean miners<br>• Survivors' Tales<br>(L) Solo sailing<br>• Extreme Sports<br>• Thrill Seekers | • Sentence adverbs<br>• Intonation: warnings |

*page 32* **Functional Language:** giving warnings *page 33* **Speaking Task:** being supportive
*page 153* **Writing Bank:** a travel blog

*page 34* **Review A**, units 1–3 *page 37* **Bring It Together** 1, 2 & 3

| | Grammar | Vocabulary | Reading & Listening | Pronunciation |
|---|---|---|---|---|
| 4 **Reinvention** *page 38* | • Present Perfect or Past Simple?<br>• Present Perfect Simple or Continuous?<br>• Uses of the *–ing* Form | • Appearance<br>• Describing people | (R) Dramatic Career Changes<br>(L) An interview with an image consultant<br>• Discussing beauty trends<br>• Speaking a different language | • Schwa /ə/<br>• Intonation: stress problems |

*page 46* **Functional Language:** complaining *page 47* **Writing Task:** an informal e-mail

| | Grammar | Vocabulary | Reading & Listening | Pronunciation |
|---|---|---|---|---|
| 5 **Food for Thought** *page 48* | • Future Forms<br>• Clauses<br>• Future Continuous<br>• Future Perfect | • Food<br>• Business | (R) On Track for a Fast Food World<br>(L) The Future of Food<br>• An interview about overfishing | • Double contractions<br>• Intonation: stress |

*page 56* **Functional Language:** checking understanding *page 57* **Speaking Task:** describing a dish
*page 154* **Writing Bank:** a wiki

| | Grammar | Vocabulary | Reading & Listening | Pronunciation |
|---|---|---|---|---|
| 6 **That's Entertainment** *page 58* | • The Passive Voice<br>• *Have something done* | • Entertainment<br>• Noun building suffixes<br>• Computer games | (R) Why make a remake?<br>• Game On!<br>(L) Talking about entertainment<br>• A radio show about unusual hobbies | • Word stress<br>• Intonation: making generalizations |

*page 66* **Functional Language:** generalizing *page 67* **Writing Task:** a review

*page 68* **Review B**, units 4–6 *page 71* **Bring It Together** 4, 5 & 6

*page 140* **Grammar Reference** *page 152* **Writing Bank** *page 155* **Communication Bank**
*page 157* **Transcripts**

# 1 Social Networks

**1** **a** Work in pairs. Look at the images. Answer the questions.

1 What situations do the images show?
2 What do they have in common?
3 Who do you spend most of your time with: friends, family or people at work?

**b** Work in pairs. Complete **A** in the **Key Vocabulary Panel**.

**2** 1.1 Listen to six people talking about the images. Match speakers 1–6 to images a–f.

**3** Work in pairs. Complete **B** in the **Key Vocabulary Panel**.

**4** **a** Use the phrasal verbs in **B** to complete the sentences.

1 We always ________ at the station whenever we go out.
2 The only time I see my other friends is when I ________ them at the supermarket.
3 You don't have to come every week, you can just ________ whenever you like.
4 I think he'd like to ________ me ________, but he's kind of shy!
5 When I ________ with my last boyfriend, I thought I'd never meet another nice guy.
6 I ________ really well with all the guys on the team.

**b** Listen to 1.1 again and check.

e

f

**5** Work in pairs. Discuss the questions.

- Where do you usually meet up with your friends? Why?
- Do you have any friends who always show up late? Does this annoy you? Why/Why not?
- When did you last run into someone you know? Were you glad to see him/her?
- Do you know anyone who has broken up recently? What are the most common reasons for people breaking up?
- Who do you get along with best: friends or family members? Why?

## Key Vocabulary

### Relationships

#### A People you know

- Describe the difference between the words in each pair. Use a dictionary to help you.

1 boss / manager
2 parents / parents-in-law
3 acquaintance / stranger
4 passenger / passerby
5 coworker or colleague / teammate
6 couple / partner
7 close friend / best friend
8 roommate / classmate

- Answer the questions about pairs of words 1–8.

1 Which ones can you match to the people in the images?
2 Do any of the words apply to you?
3 Which words relate to...
   a people who are close / not close to you?
   b people you live with / see when you go out?
   c people you work or study with / spend your free time with?

**Notice** *ex-*

We often put *ex-* before relationship nouns when we no longer have that relationship with the person:

*ex-boyfriend/girlfriend, ex-colleague, ex-boss, ex-roommate, ex-father-in-law*

#### B Phrasal verbs

- Match the phrasal verbs in the box to definitions 1–6. Use a dictionary to help you.

| ask out | get along (with) | meet up (with) |
|---|---|---|
| run into | break up (with) | show up |

1 invite someone to go somewhere, etc., because you want to start a relationship with them
2 separate (from someone), end a relationship
3 meet by accident
4 have a friendly relationship (with someone)
5 arrive, appear
6 get together to go somewhere else

# 1.1 A Window on Your World

■ Practice auxiliary verbs
■ Talk about profile pictures

a

c

b

## Speaking

**1 a** Work in pairs and look at the images. They are all profile photos on social networking sites. What do you think they say about the person who posted them?

**b** Do you have a personal profile photo? If so, what does it say about you? If not, what photo would you use? Why?

**2** Look at photo b. Answer the questions.

- Do you think it's a good profile photo? Why/Why not?
- Where do you think it was taken?
- Why do you think she chose it?

## Listening

**1 a** 1.2 Suzanne has a web page with a weekly podcast. Listen to the introduction and check your ideas in **Speaking 2**.

**b** 1.3 Listen to the rest of Suzanne's podcast. Number photos a, c and d in the order in which she talks about them.

**2 a** Work in pairs. Can you remember the answers to the questions?

1 Why didn't Jacques post a photo of himself?
2 What did he do at the Eiffel Tower?
3 Where were Dave and Suzanne when the photo was taken?
4 What happened to the man in the blue T-shirt that day?
5 Who took the photo of Gina?
6 Who can look at Gina's photos online?

**b** Listen again and check.

## Grammar

**1 a** Complete the extracts from the audio with the correct form of *be*, *have* or *do*. Leave one blank empty.

1
S This is an interesting photo—it's your profile photo, .................... it? But why .................... you use one of yourself?
J Well, I .................... think about it, but I felt a little shy, especially because I .................... changed a lot since college.

2
S I .................... seen this photo before.
D You .................... seen it—you're in it! That's you in the middle! .................... you remember?
S Oh yeah, I .................... !

3
D He climbed a tree on a dare and fell out on the way down.
S Oh, yes! He .................... hurt himself though, .................... he?

4
S Well, everyone .................... look like they .................... having fun. So... who .................... took the photo?
G My sister-in-law .................... .

**b** 1.4 Listen and check your answers.

d

**2** Read the GRAMMAR PANEL. Complete 1–5 with examples from 1a.

**3 a** Complete the questions with an auxiliary verb in the correct place. Which two questions do not need an auxiliary?

1. Are you on a social networking site? How long you been on it?
2. You've met all your online friends, you?
3. Have people ever posted photos of you online without asking? How you feel about this?
4. Which of your friends posts the most photos online?
5. You don't worry about who sees your online photos, you?
6. What happens if I google your name?

**b** Work in pairs. Answer the questions in 3a. Remember to use the auxiliary in short answers.

## PRONUNCIATION: Emphatic stress

**1 a** 1.5 Listen to sentences 1–3. Are the words in bold stressed or unstressed?

1. I **did** think about it, but I felt a little shy.
2. You **have** seen it—you're in it!
3. Yes, something **did** happen.

**b** Read Transcript 1.3 on page 162. Which sentence in 1a...

1. contradicts something that was said before?
2. confirms that something is true?
3. says that the speaker changed his/her mind?

**2** Listen again. Practice saying the sentences with the correct stress.

**3 a** Write two statements and responses with emphatic stress.

*You never post photos online.*
*I do post photos. Look at my Facebook page!*

**b** In pairs, practice reading your exchanges.

### AUXILIARY VERBS

We use auxiliary verbs...

1 to form some tenses:
*be: They're talking about profile photos.*
*have:* (1) ..........

2 to form the negative:
*I don't remember him.*

3 in *Yes/No* questions and short answers. The auxiliary verb always comes before the subject in questions:
(2) ..........

In short answers, use the pronoun + auxiliary:
*Yes, I have. No, he didn't.*

4 in object questions:
*What did you do?* (*What* is the object of the question, *you* is the subject.)
(3) ..........

**NOTE**: in subject questions, we do not use a pronoun or *do, does, did*.
*Who took the photo?* NOT *Who ~~did they take~~ the photo?*

Sometimes we use an auxiliary in short answers to *wh-* questions too:
*Who took the photo? My sister did.*

5 in question tags. We form question tags with an auxiliary verb and a pronoun. They usually follow this rule:

+ statement, – tag *You sold tickets, didn't you?*
– statement, + tag (4) ..........

6 to add emphasis to the main verb:
(5) ..........

**NOTE**: *do/does/did* are always followed by the infinitive:
*Everyone does look like they're having fun!*
NOT *Everyone does looks...*

*See page 140 for grammar reference and more practice.*

## SPEAKING

**1** Work in small groups. Discuss the questions.

- Imagine you're putting together a photo gallery about your everyday life to post online. What kind of photos would you include? What would they tell people about you?

# 1.2 Broad Banned!

- Practice past participles
- Talk about banning websites

## Speaking

**1** Work in groups. Look at the images and answer the questions.

1. Do you know all these websites? What do people use them for?
2. Do you use any of these websites? If so, which ones? How often? Which is your favorite? If not, why not?
3. All these websites have been banned by a government or an organization. Can you guess why?

## Reading

**1** **a** Read the article and check your ideas in **Speaking** question 3.

**b** According to the article, in which countries were these websites banned?

1 Facebook 2 Flickr 3 MySpace 4 YouTube

**2** Read the article again and answer the questions.

1. What kind of criminals were Twitter users protecting?
2. Why did Turkey change its mind about the ban?
3. Why has there been a mixed response to YouTube by the Russian authorities?
4. How much time were workers spending on Facebook at Portsmouth Council?

**3** Work in groups. Discuss the questions.

- Do you think it was the right decision to ban the websites? Why/Why not?
- Should governments control the Internet, or should it be available to everyone?
- What other risks can you think of in completely open access to Internet sites?

## Broad Banned!

We normally associate the Internet with freedom of expression and open access to information. However, it seems that now many countries have run out of patience with the unrestricted freedoms of the web.

In Mexico, the government has been thinking of banning the instant-messaging site Twitter. It seems that some people are disclosing the location of police traps for drunk drivers by writing "tweets." These messages warn drivers about where the police are lying in wait.

Another site to suffer from this is Flickr. The popular photo-sharing website is used by both professional and amateur photographers. This makes it difficult to control, and some inappropriate images appear there. One country that decided to act against the site is the United Arab Emirates. Its citizens were forbidden from accessing the site for five years.

File sharing of video and music has been a huge problem for the entertainment industry. Many younger people have never even bought a CD and expect to get music free online. One of the most popular sites for sharing music is MySpace. The number of uploaded tracks on the site is always increasing. In 2009, Turkey finally took action against the site, prohibiting users from accessing it. However, once the news of the ban had spread, many local musicians protested because they use MySpace to promote their songs. Fortunately, the ban ended very quickly once discussions were held between MySpace and the authorities.

YouTube has also been banned in several different countries. Despite the fact that the then Russian president had a channel on the site, YouTube was eventually banned by a Russian court in 2010 for showing videos by an extreme right-wing political organization.

Another website has had its activities stopped, not by central government, but by an ordinary

## GRAMMAR

**1 a** Work in pairs. Which websites from the article do the words in bold refer to?

a **Another website** has had its activities stopped… by an ordinary company.
b **The popular photo-sharing website** is used by both professional and amateur photographers.
c It had learned they were using **the site** for more than 400 hours a month!
d The number of uploaded tracks on **the site** is always increasing.

**b** Underline the past participle(s) in each sentence in 1a.

**2** Complete 1–4 in the GRAMMAR PANEL with the sentences in 1a.

**3** Look at the article again and answer the questions.

1 Underline three other past participles. Which uses 1–4 do they match?
2 Are the past participles regular or irregular?

**4 a** Complete the sentences with the correct form of the verbs in parentheses.

1 I ................ my password ................ once, and someone else started using my e-mail account! *(steal)*
2 I ................................ a computer virus in my life. *(never/have)*
3 My website ................................ by lots of people every week. *(visit)*
4 All the music on my MP3 player is from albums ................................ from the Internet. *(download)*

**b** Work in pairs. Discuss the sentences in 4a. Are they true for you or anyone you know?

company. In Portsmouth in the UK the local council decided to prevent its employees from using Facebook. It had learned they were using the site for more than 400 hours a month! Although the managers don't know whether users are logging on during work hours or while on their breaks, they have decided that enough is enough.

It seems that governments, websites and individuals will continue to struggle for many years to decide who really controls the Internet. The question is, how long will governments continue trying to hold back the tidal wave of online content before they give up the fight for good?

### PAST PARTICIPLES

The past participle of regular verbs is made by adding *-ed* to the infinitive.

There are also many irregular past participles, e.g., *eaten, seen, taken* (see page 168 for a full list of common ones).

#### Uses

We use the past participle…

1 with *have* to form the present perfect and past perfect tenses:
*I've finally signed up with Facebook.*
(1) ................................................

2 with *be* and a verb in the passive voice:
*He was sent an e-mail by a stranger.*
(2) ................................................

3 as adjectives:
*This is our new, improved website.*
(3) ................................................

4 with *have* in sentences that show someone does an action to or for you, e.g., when you pay someone for a service:
*He's (has) had his hair cut.*

5 or when something bad happens to you:
*I had my car stolen.*
(4) ................................................

*See page 140 for grammar reference and more practice.*

### NOTICE *LEARNED/LEARNT*

A small group of verbs have two alternative past simple / past participle forms: *-ed* is more common in American English and *-t* in British English, e.g., *learned/learnt*. Other verbs in this group are: *burn*, *dream*, *lean* and *spill*.
*Oh no, you've spilled coffee everywhere.*

## SPEAKING

**1 a** Work in groups. Think of two reasons for these opinions and two against.

1 Companies should check the Internet activity of every employee once a week.
2 People who illegally download movies, music or videos should have their Internet access blocked.
3 Criminals like drunk drivers should have their photos posted on a police website so that everyone knows who they are.
*One reason against this is that it could encourage a hate campaign against the person.*

**b** Compare your ideas with those of other groups. Do you have similar opinions?

# 1.3 FRIENDS: THE NEW FAMILY?

- PRACTICE REFLEXIVE PRONOUNS
- TALK ABOUT FAMILY & FRIENDS

## SPEAKING

**1** Work in pairs. What do the images show? What do they have in common? How do you think the people feel?

**2** **a** Match the statements to images a–d.

1 Parents' experience and knowledge can be useful for their children.
2 Teens have more fun with their friends than with their family.
3 Teens are more likely to talk about problems with friends than with their parents.
4 Different generations of a family usually get along well together.

**b** Do you agree or disagree with each statement? Give reasons for your answers.

## LISTENING

**1** **a** 1.6 Listen to an interview on a student radio program. Write Craig (C) or Marcela (M) for opinions 1 and 2.

1 Families are still the most important social unit.
2 Friends are the new family.

**b** Listen to Craig again and mark the points he mentions.

1 spending more time with friends than with family ..............
2 finding friends through work ..............
3 discussing relationships ..............
4 having the same interests ..............
5 having fun and socializing ..............
6 going on vacation together ..............
7 making friends online ..............

**2** Listen to Marcela again and answer the questions.

1 Where do Marcela's parents and other relatives live?
2 How long do children usually live with parents in her home country?
3 How many good friends does Marcela have?

**3** Work in pairs. Are you more like Craig or Marcela? Why?

a

b

c

d

## VOCABULARY: Phrasal verbs

**1** Look at the phrasal verbs from Transcript 1.6. Match verbs 1–8 to meanings a–h.

1 I **hang out** much more with friends...
2 I can always **count on** my good friends.
3 When I decided to break up with my girlfriend... I **talked** it **over** with a couple of friends first...
4 When I **go away**... it's usually with friends.
5 I often fight with my brother, but we always **make up**...
6 He can **take care of** himself...
7 I had problems in college, and I **dropped out** for a while...
8 I **took up** Pilates recently...

a leave an educational institution before you finish or earn a degree
b spend time with someone or in a place
c look after someone or something
d start a new interest or activity
e discuss a problem or plan
f leave home for a period of time, especially for a vacation
g depend on someone to do what you want or expect
h become friends again after an argument

**2** **a** Write two true and two false statements about yourself using the phrasal verbs in 1.

**b** Work in pairs. Read your sentences to your partner. He/She guesses if they are true or false.

## GRAMMAR

**1** **a** Read sentences 1–3. Cross out one extra word in each sentence.

1 We really enjoy us ourselves going to the beach and parties.
2 He can take him care of himself.
3 Sometimes I ask to myself if my relationship with my family has changed now that I'm older.

**b** Complete 1–6 in the GRAMMAR PANEL with words from 1a.

**2** **a** Complete the sentences with a reflexive pronoun.

1 Hi, come in! Make ............ at home.
2 I'm not going to behave differently. I'm just going to be ............ .
3 No one else is going to clean up. We'll have to do it ............ .
4 Don't worry. The computer can solve that problem by ............ .
5 When Isabel wants to learn new words, she says them over and over to ............ .

**b** What do you think the people in 2a are doing?

**3** Work in pairs. Answer the questions.

- When might you send yourself an e-mail?
- When was the last time your friends invited themselves over to your house?
- Have you ever accidentally hurt yourself?
- Do you know anyone who taught himself/herself to do something, e.g., to speak a language?
- When there's a problem with your home, do you fix it yourself or pay someone else to do it?

### REFLEXIVE PRONOUNS

We use reflexive pronouns when the subject and object in a sentence are the same person or thing:

*Sarah really enjoyed herself at the party.*

| | |
|---|---|
| I | (1) ............ |
| you | yourself/yourselves |
| he | (2) ............ |
| she | herself |
| it | itself |
| we | (3) ............ |
| they | themselves |

#### Verbs with reflexive pronouns

Common verbs that go with reflexive pronouns are:

(4) ............ , *blame*, (5) ............ , *express*, *give*, *hurt*, *introduce*, (6) ............ and *teach*.

*See page 140 for grammar reference and more practice.*

### NOTICE OFFERS & ORDERS

We also use reflexive pronouns to make offers:

*Help yourself!*

or to give orders:

*Do it yourself!*

## SPEAKING

**1** **a** Work in pairs. Talk about the time you spend with friends and family. Take notes on your partner's opinions and experiences as you listen. Find out...

- if he/she lives with his/her family
- who he/she looks to for support with problems
- what kind of relationship he/she has with family and friends
- whether he/she agrees that friends are the new family.

**b** Report your findings to the class. Are there any similarities?

## Tune In

**1** Read the definition. What is the link to the image?

> **small talk** conversations about unimportant topics. You *make small talk* when you meet people that you don't know very well.

**2** Make a list of topics that you would/wouldn't talk about with people you don't know well.

*I wouldn't talk about politics because it can be very controversial.*

**3** **a** 1.7 Listen to six people making small talk. Number the topics in the order they talk about them. There is one extra topic.

| | | | |
|---|---|---|---|
| family | ........ | sports | ........ |
| vacations | ........ | the weather | ........ |
| people they know | ........ | food | ........ |
| politics | ........ | | |

**b** Which conversation 1–6 does the image show?

## Focus on Language

**4** **a** 1.8 Complete sentences 1–6 from the audio. Listen and check.

1 I'm not really a big ........ ........ to be honest.
2 I took a ........ to ........ once.
3 I think you've ........ the ........ with you!
4 Speaking of ........ , I think I'll get something to ........ .
5 She's the girl with the ........ ........ , isn't she?
6 I have a ........ of them. Would you ........ to see it?

**b** Match sentences 1–6 in 4a to functions a–f.

a changing the subject
b making an offer
c discussing people you know
d finding something in common with the other speaker
e politely rejecting the topic
f talking about the weather

### Question tags

1.9 Listen to three sentences. Does the intonation rise or fall on the question tags?

1 That was a great game last night, wasn't it?
2 You don't come from Watten, do you?
3 She's the girl with the red hair, isn't she?

Complete the rules. Listen again and check.

Intonation in question tags ........ when we're sure about the statement and we think the listener will agree.

It ........ when we're not sure about the statement.

Practice saying sentences 1–3 with the correct intonation.

## Over to You

**5** Work in pairs. Imagine you are in these situations and you do not know the person next to you. Think of one "small talk" phrase for each.

1 You're on a long-haul flight from your country to Tokyo.
2 You're at a dinner party at your boss's house.
3 You're a tourist on a one-day sightseeing tour of New York.
4 It's your first day of class. You're on a coffee break with the other students.

**6** **a** Change partners. Act out two of the conversations in 5. How long can you keep the conversation going?

**b** Work with your partner from 5. Which conversation was more successful? Why?

## TUNE IN

**1** Work in pairs. Look at the image of Carl, who shares an apartment with Lydia. Answer the questions.

1 Where is he?
2 What do you think has happened?
3 What other problems do roommates often have with each other?

**2** **a** 1.10 Listen to Carl telling his friend Denise about Lydia. Does he mention any of your ideas in 1?

**b** Listen again. Underline and correct the false information in each sentence.

1 Well, the thing is, she's really messy.
2 She's always forgetting to take the trash out when she leaves.
3 She forgets to buy things like cheese or fruit, even when I ask her to.
4 Every time I try to talk to her, she just walks away.
5 She won't wash the dishes unless I ask her to.

**3** **a** Carl asks Denise for advice. What suggestions do you think she gives him?

**b** 1.11 Listen and check your ideas.

## PREPARE FOR TASK

**4** **a** Complete Denise's suggestions 1–5 with the phrases in the box.

One other thing you could do / I'm not sure / You could always / I suppose / I think in that case

1 .................... , but I think talking always helps.
2 .................... , you have to get angry with her.
3 .................... you could do your shopping separately.
4 .................... is put a list of jobs on the refrigerator door with people's names next to each one.
5 .................... try complaining about her on Facebook.

**b** Listen to 1.11 again and check.

**5** Work in pairs. Which of Denise's suggestions is the best? Are any of them bad ideas? Why?

**6** **a** What advice could you give in these situations? Make one suggestion for each, using language from 4a.

1 Your friend always comes to visit you without warning, and then you have to chat with him/her for hours.
2 You've started a new job. Your coworkers often go for lunch together, but they never invite you.
3 Your boss often gives you work at 5 p.m. on Friday afternoon, and she wants it finished by Monday morning.

**b** Compare your suggestions with a partner's. Were any of them the same?

## TASK

**7** **a** Work in pairs. Choose one of the situations. Then read the instructions for Student A and Student B, and choose a role.

**Situation 1** One of your friends is always late when you meet up or changes the plan at the last minute.

**Situation 2** One of your coworkers is really messy and is always leaving dirty plates and cups on his desk.

**Student A** Explain what the problem is. Don't accept a suggestion unless you think it's a really good one.
**Student B** Keep offering suggestions until Student A accepts one.

**b** Plan three things that you want to say in your role.

**8** Act out your situation in 7a. Then exchange roles and act out the other situation.

## REPORT BACK

**9** Present the best or most unusual solution from 8 to the class. The class votes on the best solution.

➜ Go to Review A, Unit 1, p. 34 ➜ Go to Writing Bank 1, p. 152

# 2 EXPERTS

a

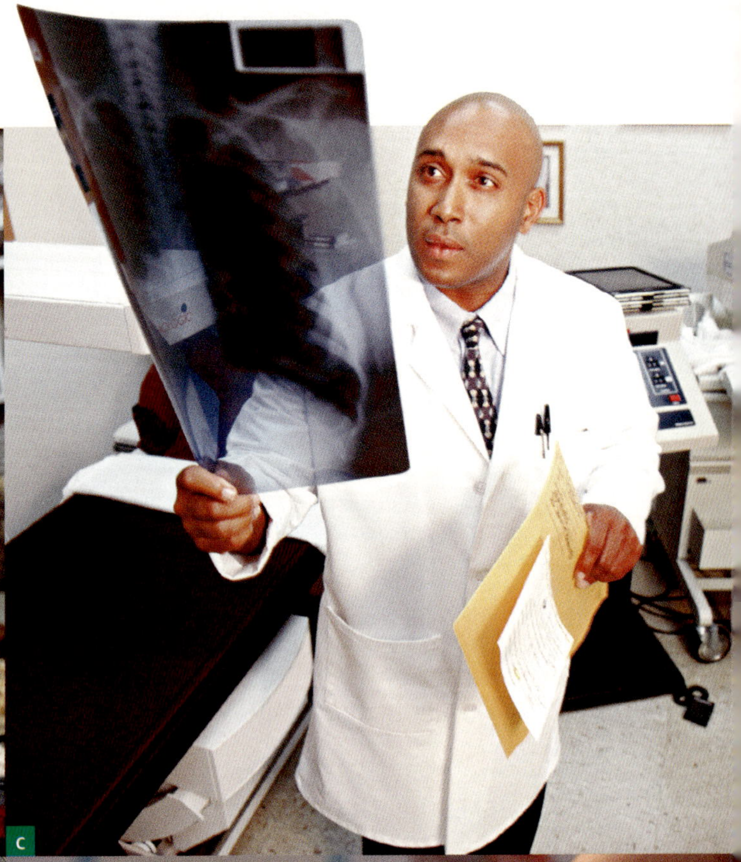

c

b

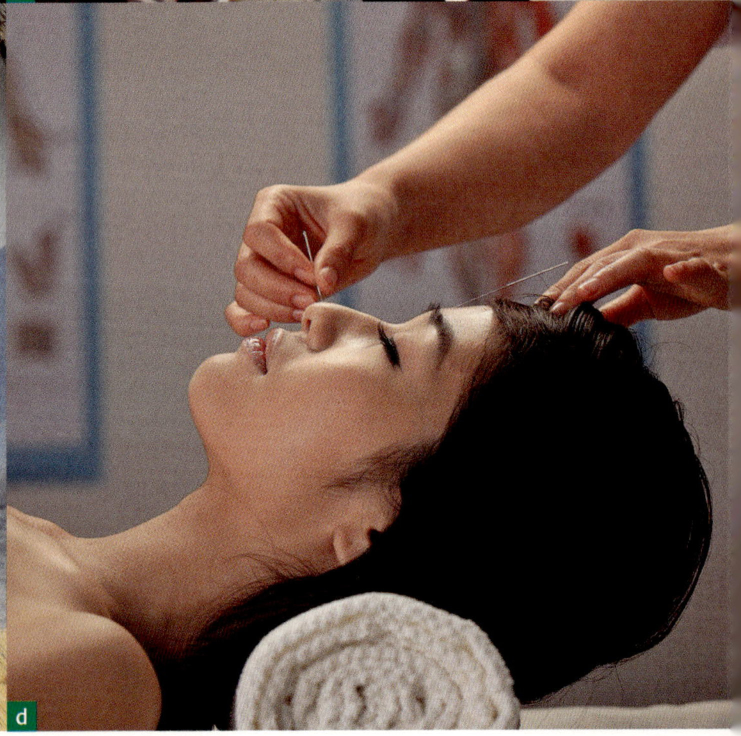

d

**1 a** Work in pairs. Look at the images and answer the questions.

1 What do they have in common? What's the connection with the title of the unit?
2 What countries do you think they were taken in?

**b** Are the treatments in the images available in your country? Which are considered...
a) traditional? b) conventional? c) alternative?

2 a Work in pairs. Complete A in the KEY VOCABULARY PANEL. Use a dictionary to help you.

b Work in groups. Answer the questions.

1 Which of the medical experts in A do you trust the most? Why?
2 Which of the experts have you used/consulted?

3 a 2.1 Listen to three people talking about health issues. Match speakers 1–3 to statements a–c.

a She thinks there's a place for conventional medicine and natural remedies.
b She believes conventional medicine is still the best option.
c She's in favor of alternative medicine.

b Why do the speakers have these opinions?

4 Work in pairs. Complete B in the KEY VOCABULARY PANEL.

5 a Complete the sentences from Transcript 2.1 with words from A and B in the KEY VOCABULARY PANEL.

1 When I get a cold or the flu, I take ________ or ________ .
2 If I get an ________ , I usually take ________ .
3 I use an ________ for problems such as a stomachache, a cold or the flu.
4 My dad gets ________ a lot, and he swears by his ________ .
5 I get a flu ________ every winter, but I use arnica cream on a ________ or ________ .

b Listen to 2.1 again and check.

6 Work in pairs. Complete C in the KEY VOCABULARY PANEL.

7 Work in groups. Answer the questions.

1 What do you usually do if you feel sick?
   a Check the symptoms online.
   b Go to the doctor.
   c Go to a homeopath or acupuncturist.
2 What treatment do you take for these symptoms or illnesses?
   a a cold or the flu
   b a backache
   c a headache
   d a rash
   e insomnia
3 Which type of medicine do you think is most effective? Why?

## KEY VOCABULARY

### Health

### A Medical experts

- Which of the words in the box can you match to the images?

acupuncturist chiropractor herbalist homeopath midwife nurse pharmacist shaman specialist surgeon

### B Symptoms & treatment

- Look at the words in the box. Which describe a) symptoms? b) a form of treatment? Use a dictionary to help you, if necessary.

antibiotics backache bruise bump cough syrup infection injection insomnia operation painkillers rash temperature vaccination

- How many of the words are similar in your language?

### C Collocations

- Match verbs 1–7 to nouns a–g to make common collocations from the audio.

| | |
|---|---|
| 1 take | a medicine |
| 2 feel/be | b an appointment |
| 3 take someone's | c side effects |
| 4 make | d a prescription |
| 5 write | e ill/well/sick |
| 6 treat | f an illness/symptoms |
| 7 have | g temperature |

**NOTICE** *GET*

It is very common to use the verb *get* to talk about health. It can mean:

*become*: *get sick/well*
*receive*: *get a vaccination*
*catch/be affected by*: *get an infection/a backache*

- PRACTICE THE PRESENT TENSES
- TALK ABOUT STAYING IN SHAPE

## SPEAKING

**1** Work in groups. Look at the images. What aspects of health and fitness do they show?

**2** **a** Match aspects of fitness 1–6 to images a–d. Use a dictionary to help you.

1 a personal trainer
2 a regular workout
3 a couch potato
4 diet pills/supplements
5 junk food
6 gentle exercise

**b** What are the most popular ways to stay in shape in your country? What do you do to stay in shape?

## READING

**1** Read the article. Which image a–d <u>isn't</u> talked about?

**2** Match summary sentences a–e to paragraphs 1–5.

a Enthusiasm for working out often runs out quickly.
b You can exercise in many different ways.
c Joining a fitness center is a popular activity.
d You can increase motivation by doing something you enjoy.
e Many people hope to lose weight without making an effort.

**3** Read the article again and answer the questions.

1 What do gyms depend on to make money?
2 Why is it easy to persuade people to buy weight loss products?
3 What advice does the article give people who don't like doing regular exercise?
4 Why does Kay like ballet barre?

**4** Work in small groups. Discuss the questions.

- Does any of the information in the article surprise you? Why/Why not?
- Is the situation similar in your country?
- What other ideas can you think of to help people get in better shape without getting bored?

a

b

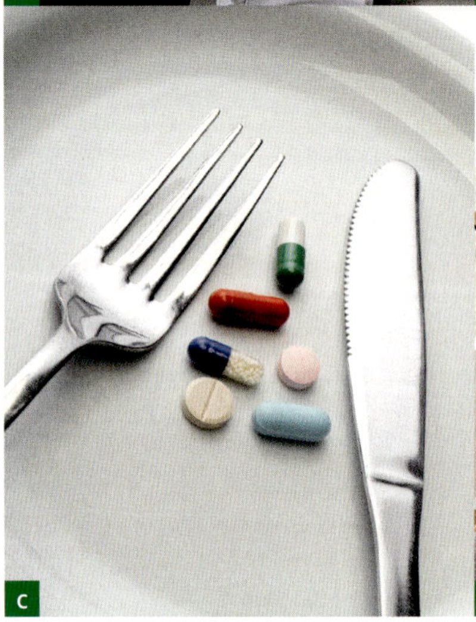
c

d

# Putting the Fun...

**1** It's that time of year when millions of people decide to sign up for the gym in an enthusiastic attempt to get in shape. Gym membership and sports clothing and equipment are multimillion dollar industries. Personal trainers are the latest thing for gym goers and classes such as Pilates, spinning, Zumba and tae bo have replaced aerobics as the fashionable exercise of choice.

**2** Yet despite the millions we spend on gym membership and fitness classes each year, motivation often slips, and the workout sessions soon stop. And yet we continue to pay! A recent study found that in the UK alone people waste a total of $60 million a year on unused gym membership and sports equipment. But having good intentions that soon fade away is part of life, and it's exactly what gyms rely on to make money.

**3** While the fitness industry in the USA is worth $17.6 billion a year, the diet and weight loss industry is worth more than double this: $46 billion! People spend millions on weight loss products such as diet pills, creams, slimming gadgets and self-help books. Pseudo experts are always showing products

## GRAMMAR

**1 a** Read the sentences from the article. Do the sentences talk about the past, present or future? What tense is used in each one?

1 People spend millions on weight loss products.
2 Pseudo experts are always showing products on TV to help you lose weight.
3 I've tried the gym.
4 I'm taking a class called "ballet barre."
5 I often go before work.
6 I'm getting better each week.
7 The class starts next month.

**b** Complete 1–7 in the GRAMMAR PANEL with the sentences in 1a.

**2 a** Complete the sentences with the correct form of the verbs in parentheses.

1 I .................... to the gym twice a week. *(usually/go)*
2 My friend .................... a yoga class at the moment. *(take)*
3 My mom .................... me to eat more fruit and vegetables. It's so annoying! *(always/tell)*
4 I can't wait to take the new kickboxing course. It .................... in May. *(start)*
5 I .................... a squash club. I couldn't play at first but now I .................... slowly. *(join/improve)*

**b** Work in pairs. Change the sentences in 2a so they are true for you or someone you know.

### THE PRESENT

**Present simple**

We use the present simple to talk about...
1 habits and routines:
(1) ....................
2 things that are generally true:
(2) ....................
3 schedules and timetables:
(3) ....................

**Present continuous**

We use the present continuous...
1 to talk about things that are happening now or in a period around now:
(4) ....................
2 to talk about changing or developing situations:
(5) ....................
3 with *always* to talk about annoying habits:
(6) ....................

**Present perfect**

We use the present perfect to talk about actions that started in the past and have a result/relevance in the present:
(7) ....................

*See page 141 for grammar reference and more practice.*

# Back into Fitness

on TV to help you lose weight. These scams promise great results without the need to do any exercise or even modify your diet, which of course is why they are so appealing.

4 But what alternatives are there if you feel sick at the idea of working out every day but guilty if you don't set aside time to fulfill the minimum exercise quota? The trick is to stay active without feeling you have to schedule a time and stick to a routine. Walking the dog, gardening, dancing and playing with children all count as exercise if you do them regularly.

5 But the most important thing of all is to find something that you love and genuinely look forward to. Fitness enthusiast Kay says, "I've tried the gym, but it's so boring and repetitive I don't go anymore. At the moment I'm taking a class called 'ballet barre,' which is a workout through ballet exercises. I often go before work. The combination of dance and a tough workout is really motivating—I'm loving it! I'm learning a new skill, and I'm getting better each week. I enjoy it so much I'm going to take up classical ballet, too. The class starts next month—I can't wait!"

### NOTICE *I'M LOVING IT!*

In informal English people sometimes use *like/love* (in the sense of "enjoy") and *hate* in the present continuous:
*I'm loving the course!* but NOT ~~*I'm loving you*~~.
*I'm hating my new job.*

## SPEAKING

**1 a** Work in groups. What would you introduce in schools in your country to help children stay in shape and be healthy?
*a free bike service, ban junk food from school lunches...*

**b** Share your ideas with the class. Which group has the best ideas?

a

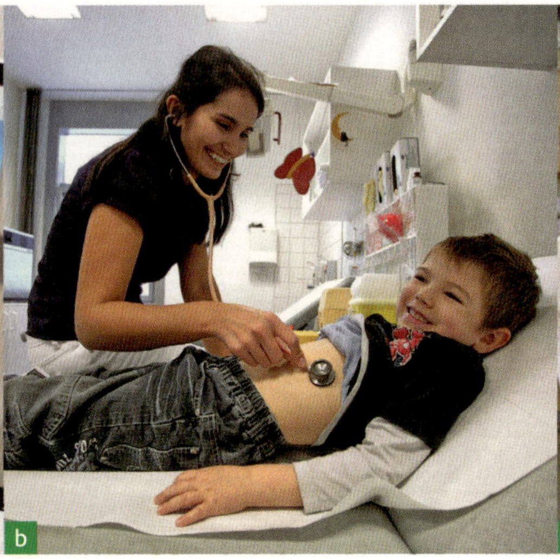
b

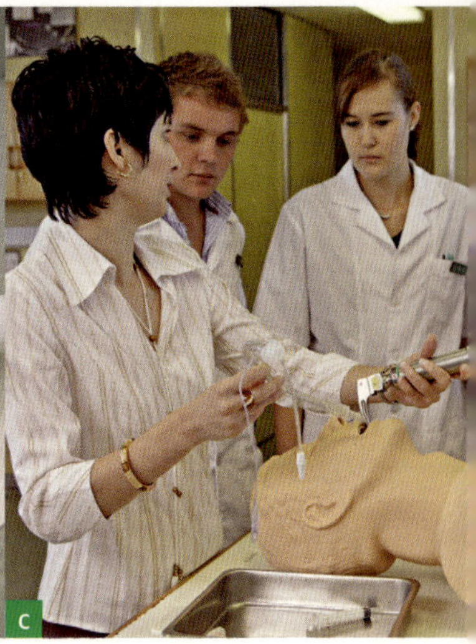
c

## SPEAKING

**1** Work in groups. Discuss the questions.

1 Look at the images. What aspect of medicine does each one show?
2 Are any of your classmates doctors or studying to be doctors? If so, what are their specializations?
3 What skills do you need to be a doctor?

## LISTENING

**1** 2.2 Listen to an interview with Laura, a Mexican doctor, talking about her medical career. Number images a–d in the order she talks about them.

**2** Listen again and mark the topics that Laura mentions.

1 her home life and family ..............
2 her medical training and specialization ..............
3 the role of traditional healers in the community ..............
4 the most common illnesses that she treats ..............
5 changes in the information patients can access nowadays ..............
6 her favorite and least favorite aspect of being a doctor ..............

**3** Are the sentences true or false? Correct the false sentences.

1 Laura decided to become a doctor mainly because she liked science subjects in school.
2 To qualify as a pediatrician, she earned a four-year degree and did a year of social service and a year of residency.
3 She did her social service in an isolated rural area.
4 Local people used the clinic a lot when they had medical problems.
5 She's against the use of traditional medicine.
6 The parents of her patients often think they know more about the problem than she does.

## VOCABULARY: Medicine

**1** **a** Look at Transcript 2.2 on page 162. Which of these words can you find?

1 pediatrician paramedic
2 patient surgeon
3 nurse midwife
4 ward operating room
5 bandage Band-Aid
6 self-diagnosis self-medication

**b** Work in pairs. Explain the difference between the pairs of words in 1a. Use a dictionary to help you.

**2** Work in pairs. Discuss the questions.

- Are you a good patient? Why/Why not?
- Which would you prefer to be, a midwife or a surgeon? Why?
- What are the advantages or disadvantages of self-diagnosis and self-medication?

## GRAMMAR

**1** **a** Work in pairs. Read sentences a–d. Underline all the examples of *used to*.

a I used to work as an assistant to a paramedic.
b I wasn't used to living in such a small community.
c In the beginning it was frustrating, but now I'm getting used to it.
d Doctors are more used to dealing with this situation these days.

**b** Answer the questions about the sentences in 1a.

1 Which sentences talk about a) the present? b) the past?
2 Which sentences talk about…
   a a past habit, state or situation?
   b a situation that is becoming normal?
   c a situation that was strange/unfamiliar in the past?

**2** Read sections A and B in the GRAMMAR PANEL and complete 1–6.

**3** Complete the sentences with the correct *used to* expression and the verbs in parentheses. Where do you think the speakers are in each sentence?

1 I'm still not .................... to .................... spicy food. *(eat)*
2 I'm .................... to .................... my shoes off in people's houses, but I still forget sometimes. *(take)*
3 When I first arrived, I .................... to .................... friends so late at night, but now it seems normal. *(meet)*
4 I didn't .................... to .................... by waterbus when I lived there. *(travel)*
5 I'll never .................... to .................... on the wrong side of the street. *(drive)*
6 Did you .................... to .................... to the beach on weekends? *(go)*

**4** **a** Write a true sentence for each situation. Think of something...

1 you used to believe as a child.
2 you're getting used to but is still difficult.
3 you'll never get used to.
4 you weren't used to at one time but now is fine.
5 you've slowly gotten used to over the years.

**b** Work in pairs. Discuss your answers in 4a. Are there any similarities?

*I'll never get used to wearing a suit to work.*
*Me either. It's so uncomfortable.*

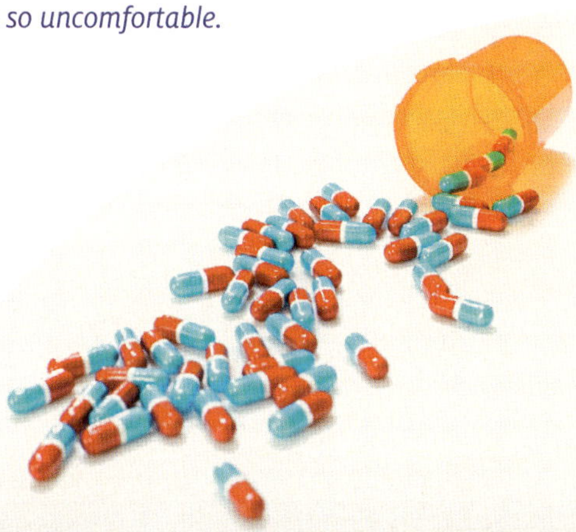

## USED TO DO/USED TO DOING

### A Used to

We use ***used to*** + the (1) .................... to talk about situations, habits or repeated actions in the past. Often they are things we no longer do:

\+ *I* (2) .................... *to live in Paris.*
– *I didn't use to speak French.*
? *Did you* (3) .................... *to eat out a lot?*
*Yes, I did./No, I didn't.*

**NOTE:**
In the negative and question forms we drop the *-d* in *used to*:
*I didn't use to speak French.* NOT *I didn't used to speak French.*

### B Be/Get used to

We use *be/get used to* + a noun/pronoun or the (4) .................... form of the verb.

We use (5) .................... *used to* to talk about things that are familiar and no longer strange to us:
*I'm used to working long hours.*

We use (6) .................... *used to* to talk about things that become less strange/difficult over time:
*I'm getting used to starting work at 8 a.m.*

*See page 141 for grammar reference and more practice.*

## PRONUNCIATION: Shifts in stress

**1** **a** Work in pairs. Read sentences 1–6. Underline the stressed syllable in the words in bold.

1 It was part of a volunteer **project**.
2 For many illnesses, they were **content** to see the *curandero*.
3 They also do ritual cleansings with herbs, eggs or other **objects**.
4 I don't **object** to traditional medicine.
5 They know the entire **contents** of the relevant Wikipedia article!
6 Sometimes I **project** an X-ray on the wall.

**b** 2.3 Listen and check. What parts of speech are the words in bold in 1a?

**2** Practice saying the sentences in 1a with the correct stress on the words in bold.

## SPEAKING

**1** Work in groups. Discuss the questions. Give reasons for your answers.

- How has information on the Internet changed the relationship between doctor and patient?
- Do you think we take too much medicine these days?
- Are we healthier than our parents or grandparents? Why/Why not?

- PRACTICE WORDS ENDING IN ...*EVER*
- TALK ABOUT EXPERIMENTS

## SPEAKING & READING

**1 a** Work in groups. Look at the first image in the article. When and where do you think it was taken? What are the people doing?

**b** Read the first paragraph of the article and check your answers to 1a. Are you surprised? Why/Why not?

**2** Read the rest of the article. What is the link between the experiment and the title of the article? Answer the questions in pairs.

1. According to the article, why did people follow the orders of the scientist in the experiment?
2. Is Wikipedia more or less inaccurate than the *Encyclopedia Britannica*? Why?
3. Why did the gold mining company ask for help online?
4. Why do university professors write for Wikipedia?
5. How were the results of the experiment different fifty years later? Does this surprise you?

**3** Fill in blanks 1–4 in the article with sentences a–d.

a They received replies from all over the world—and made $3 billion from the information!
b But instead of the man in the lab coat, a TV host gave the instructions.
c And however many people edit a Wikipedia article, professional research is always needed at the beginning.
d The idea is that, because the website is constantly being corrected, eventually the best text will be created.

**4** Work in pairs. Discuss the questions.

- How do you think the participants felt during and after Milgram's experiment?
- Why do you think the experiment has never been repeated by scientists?
- Do you use Wikipedia? If so, what kind of information do you research? If not, why not?

# We're All Experts Now

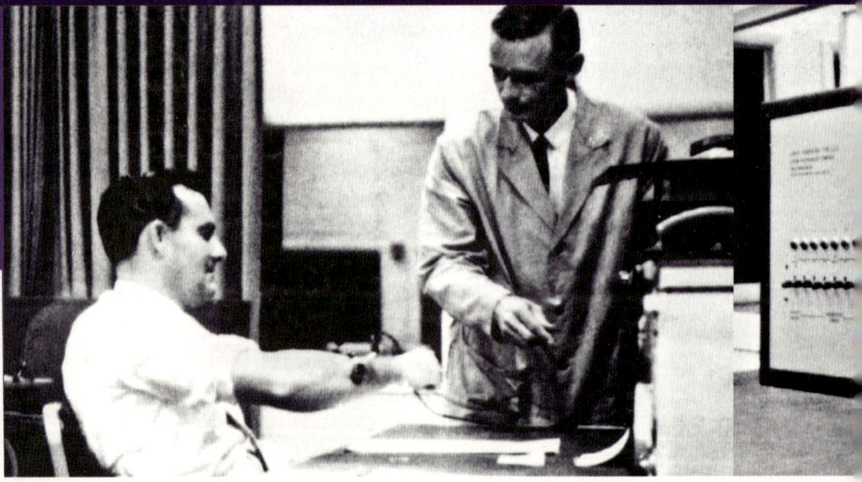

In the 1960s, American scientist Stanley Milgram invited members of the public into his laboratory. There, an "expert" in a lab coat told them to press a button that would give an electric shock to a stranger on the other side of a screen. What Milgram's subjects didn't know was that it was all fake–the stranger was just an actor. Whenever the actor answered a question incorrectly, the button was pressed. The "electric shock" became stronger each time until the actor started to scream "in pain." Encouraged by the expert, the majority of people ignored the screams and kept pressing the button, whatever the number of volts!

This seems to indicate that, in the past, people were more likely to follow the orders of experts and authority figures without question. Most people hadn't been to college, so doctors and scientists seemed to have much greater knowledge than the average person in the street. Nowadays, even specialized information can easily be obtained by whoever wants it. The line between ordinary people and experts is not so clear.

In the case of Wikipedia, the online encyclopedia, anyone can change the content of its pages. (1) .......... And it works. In 2005, the journal *Nature* compared Wikipedia articles with similar articles from the *Encyclopedia Britannica*. They discovered that whichever site you use, there is a similar number of errors, with only slightly more in Wikipedia (3.86 per article compared to 2.92).

Big businesses are realizing this, too. The Canadian mining company Goldcorp put all the information about their land online. They asked the public to tell them where they thought gold might be located–with a reward of $500,000. (2) ..........

So is it the end of the expert? Not really. Many professors are writing

## VOCABULARY: ...*ever*

**1** Look at the complete article again. Underline all the words that end in *ever*.

*Whenever,...*

**2 a** Replace the words in bold with underlined words from the article.

1 **Every time** the actor answered a question incorrectly, the button was pressed... **it didn't matter what** the number of volts **was**!
2 Nowadays, even specialized information can easily be obtained by **anyone who** wants it.
3 **It doesn't matter which** site you use, there is a similar number of errors.
4 **It doesn't matter how** much they dislike it, their students will use the site as their first point of reference.
5 **It's not important how** many people edit a Wikipedia article, professional research is always needed at the beginning.

**b** How do you say the sentences in 2a in your language?

**3 a** Complete the sentences with the words from 1.

1 .................... I want to go to a bar or restaurant, I always look for a recommendation online.
2 I always trust doctors or nurses, .................... they say. They're the professionals, aren't they?
3 When I need directions or help in a foreign city, I ask .................... is nearby and looks friendly.
4 .................... much I look for information on other websites, I always end up using Wikipedia.
5 I only ever look at one review of a movie or a book. .................... one you read, they all say the same thing.
6 .................... many soccer games I watch, I never get bored.

**b** Work in small groups. Are sentences 1–6 in 3a true for you?

### NOTICE *WHATEVER*

In informal English, people sometimes use *whatever* to dismiss what someone says and show they don't care. This use is often impolite:

*"I told you not to trust him." "Whatever!"*

We can also use it as a response to a question/suggestion to show that we don't mind:

*"Should we eat here then?" "Whatever you think."*

for Wikipedia because however much they dislike it, their students will use the site as their first point of reference. (3) .............. Goldcorp relied on experts as well, since professional geologists are also members of the public.

With the public better educated and more questioning than ever before, we would expect a different result in the Milgram experiment today. Or would we? In 2010, a French TV show repeated the experiment. (4) .............. And the result? Fifty years later, more people (80%) continued to press the button than in the original experiment (65%).

## SPEAKING

**1 a** Look at the image for one minute and then cover it. Prepare notes describing what you saw.

**b** Compare your notes with a partner's. Did you see the same things?

**2** You are going to do another simple psychology experiment. Student A, turn to page 158. Student B, turn to page 160.

## TUNE IN

**1** Work in pairs. Look at the image and answer the questions.

1 What store does it show?
2 What can you buy there?
3 Why might you go there when you are on vacation? Think of as many reasons as you can.

**2** 2.4 Listen to a tourist, Jackie, talking to a pharmacist in Egypt. Answer the questions.

1 What problem does Jackie have?
2 What solution does the pharmacist offer?

**3 a** Number the events in the order they happened.

........ The pharmacist bandages her arm.
........ The pharmacist gives her directions.
........ Jackie falls down.
........ The pharmacist examines her arm.
........ Jackie takes a photo.
........ The pharmacist tells her to go to the hospital.

**b** Listen again and check.

## FOCUS ON LANGUAGE

**4 a** Order the words in bold to complete the sentences.

1 **if wonder you I could** help me.
2 **mind you would** taking a look at it?
3 **you me tell if could** it's broken?
4 **possible it to would be** bandage it?
5 **do idea have any you** how long I'll have to wait?

**b** 2.5 Listen and check.

**5 a** How are these questions different from the questions in 4a?

- Can you help me?
- Will you take a look at it?

**b** Why didn't Jackie use questions like these?

**Stress**

2.5 Listen again to the questions in 4a. Underline the main stress.

*I wonder if you could help me.*

Listen again and repeat with the correct stress.

**6** Work in pairs. Imagine you are in a city in another country. Make one polite request for help for each situation.

1 You want to change rooms in your hotel.
2 You don't know how to use the ticket machine on the bus.
3 You're not sure which stop to get off at for the museum.
4 You want to know what time the museum closes.
5 You don't know the way to the train station.

## OVER TO YOU

**7 a** Work in pairs. Read the cards and choose a role. Act out the situation. Use as many questions from 4a as you can.

**Tourist**

You're on vacation. You notice a nasty bite on your arm, so you go to a pharmacy. Ask the pharmacist to…
- look at the bite
- recommend something for it
- tell you how often to take/use the medication
- tell you if you should see a doctor

**Pharmacist**

A tourist comes into the pharmacy with a bite on his/her arm. Find out how he/she got it and respond to his/her requests.

**b** Switch roles and act out the situation again.

## Tune In

**1** Work in pairs. Describe the person in the image. How old is she? What do you think she does?

**2** Read the question posted to a website. What advice would you give Raffaella?

**Ask the experts**

Hello world!
Can anybody help me? I'm a high school student, and I graduate at the end of this year. I want to go to college if I pass all my exams, but I'm not sure what to study. I'm interested in psychology, but I've never studied it before and don't really know anything about it. What should I do?
**Raffaella321**

**All Comments (3)**

I made some big mistakes when I chose my major in college. I started with politics, then I changed to history, and finally I dropped out altogether. It's important to know exactly what you want to do because you're committing to four years or more. My advice would be to find out as much as you can about the career online. This will help you decide whether it's what you really want to do.
**Madia007** Answer #1

You can't overestimate the importance of choosing the right major and the right college or university. Many people choose the university first, but the lecturers and facilities are probably even more important. Since many universities have open-house days, take time to visit as many as you can and talk to whoever you can while you're there. I found that really useful. It'll help you decide if both the major and the college are right.
**Hideki22** Answer #2

If I were you, I'd wait before making a final decision. If you're not sure about what to major in, don't go to college next year. Take a year off, travel and decide what you really want to do with your life. That's what I did! Whatever you do, don't rush into a decision. Of course, a year off has its good and bad points. You won't make any progress in your career during that year, but it's valuable life experience and will help you make a final decision about career.
**NaomiV** Answer #3

**3** Read the replies to Raffaella's post. Answer the questions in pairs.

1 Which reply do you think is best? Why?
2 In what ways are the people giving advice more expert than Raffaella?

## Prepare for Task

**4** **a** Match 1–6 to a–f to complete the advice.

1 It's important to
2 My advice would be
3 You can't overestimate
4 Take time
5 If I were you,
6 Whatever you do,

a the importance of choosing the right major.
b don't rush into a decision.
c to visit as many as you can.
d I'd wait before making a final decision.
e know exactly what you want to do.
f to find out as much as you can online.

**b** Read replies 1–3 again and check your answers.

**5** Work in pairs. Use phrases 1–6 in 4a to give more advice to Raffaella.

*My advice would be to find out about some other majors, too.*

## Task

**6** **a** Work in pairs. Read the blog post. Think of as much advice as possible to give "Desperate88."

Showing first 10 comments | Go to latest comment

**Desperate88** Help! I'm studying for my final exams, but I have to work part-time as well. I have no free time and I'm exhausted, but I can't sleep. I'm really worried I'm going to fail my exams.
posted at 11:42 a.m. • Like

**b** Choose the best suggestions and write a reply.

## Report Back

**7** Read your reply to the class. Answer the questions.

1 Did anyone give similar advice to yours?
2 Who gave the best advice?

➜ Go to Review A, Unit 2, p. 35 

# 3 SURVIVAL

a

b

Sixteen-year-old Jessica Watson is the youngest person to sail nonstop, solo and unassisted around the world. She sailed into Sydney harbor on May 15, seven months after setting off on a difficult and dangerous voyage. Thousands of well-wishers, including the Australian Prime Minister, turned out to welcome her. Jessica's support team said she had sailed nearly 23,000 nautical miles—that's 43,000 kilometers. However, her record has been questioned since she did not go far enough north of the Equator to claim a true circumnavigation of the globe.

**1** Work in pairs. Look at the images and answer the questions.

1 What do the images show?
2 What do you think the girl has achieved?
3 Would you like to do something like this? Why/Why not?

**2** **a** Read the article. Check your answers to question 2 in 1.

**b** What else did you find out about Jessica? How do you think she felt after the voyage?

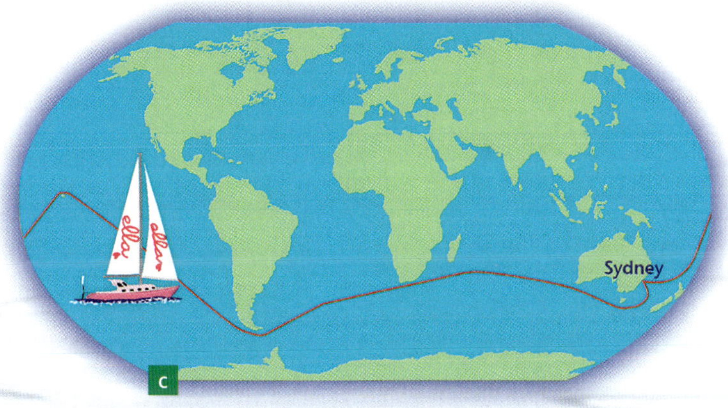


**3** 3.1 Listen to an interview with a sailing expert. Mark the topics he mentions.

| | | | |
|---|---|---|---|
| clothing | ............ | physical and psychological qualities | ............ |
| communication | ............ | safety | ............ |
| food | ............ | sleep | ............ |
| navigation | ............ | weather conditions | ............ |

**4** Work in pairs. Complete **A** in the KEY VOCABULARY PANEL. Use a dictionary to help you.

**5** **a** 3.2 Listen to two people giving their opinion about Jessica's voyage. Answer the questions.

1 Is each speaker's opinion positive or negative?
2 What do the speakers agree on?

**b** Listen again and complete **B** in the KEY VOCABULARY PANEL.

**6** Work in groups. Discuss the questions.

- What's your opinion of Jessica and her voyage?
- Have you ever been on a long or difficult trip?
- What equipment and clothing did you need?
- What difficulties did you experience?

**NOTICE** COMPOUND ADJECTIVES WITH NUMBERS

We use a singular noun in compound adjectives with numbers:

*16-year-old Jessica Watson* NOT *16-years-old*
*a ten-hour trip* NOT *a ten-hours trip*

## KEY VOCABULARY

### Survival

### A Equipment

- Answer the questions with the words in the box. Some words match more than one question.

binoculars compass first-aid kit
flashlight GPS lifeboat/life raft
life jacket radar ropes sails
thermal underwear waterproof clothing

- Which equipment do you use...

1 for survival?
2 for navigation?
3 to steer a ship/boat?
4 to see things that are far away?
5 to see in the dark?
6 for protection from extreme weather?
7 for medical problems?

### B Personality adjectives

- Mark the words you hear. Which two words are negative?

| | | | |
|---|---|---|---|
| courageous | ............ | determined | ............ |
| experienced | ............ | irresponsible | ............ |
| mature | ............ | reckless | ............ |
| resilient | ............ | resourceful | ............ |
| self-sufficient | ............ | well-prepared | ............ |

- Match the words in the box to definitions 1–10. Use a dictionary to help you.

1 takes dangerous risks
2 grown-up
3 able to provide for yourself
4 brave
5 not sensible or reasonable
6 able to recover quickly from difficult situations
7 skilled or knowledgeable
8 not letting anything stop you once you've made a decision
9 good at finding ways to deal with problems
10 organized, with everything you need for a situation

- Which adjectives describe you? Why? Which ones describe other people you know?

*My niece is very reckless. She's always climbing things and falling down.*

## SPEAKING & READING

**1** Work in pairs. Look at the image and answer the questions.

1 What news story does it come from?
2 What do you remember about this story?
3 What piece of equipment is shown? How do you think it worked?
4 What do you think was the biggest problem for a) the miners? b) the rescuers?

**2** **a** Read the article and check your answers in 1.

**b** Number the topics in the order they are mentioned.

1 conditions underground ...............
2 sending essential supplies ...............
3 rescuing the miners ...............
4 support from experts ...............
5 the miners' families ...............
6 the influence of the team leader ...............

**3** Answer the questions about the article.

1 How long were the miners trapped underground?
2 What physical problems did they have to deal with?
3 Give two examples of why Luis Urzua was an effective leader.
4 Why was the supply line so important?
5 Which experts supported the miners and the rescue efforts? How did they support them?
6 How were the miners rescued in the end?

**4** Work in groups. Discuss the questions.

- What impresses you most about this survival story?
- How do you think the miners' lives have changed?

# Celebrations as Chilean Miners Rescued

The eyes of the world were watching as the capsule brought up the last of the 33 miners from the San José mine in Chile. The men had survived underground for 69 days after a rockfall caused a tunnel to collapse. The conditions they faced were daunting. In order to survive, they had to put up with 90% humidity, avoid starvation, battle thirst and cope with constant darkness. The miners managed to set up lights to simulate day and night, and this allowed them to move around the tunnels.

Luis Urzua's role as leader was tremendously important. He had been working as a miner for 31 years before he became famous. As shift leader he had built a reputation for protecting and caring for his team. He had to convince the miners to ration two days' worth of supplies to last the 17 days before they were discovered. The miners ate one teaspoon of tuna and half a glass of milk every 48 hours. Discipline was strict. The men worked in shifts to improve conditions, and one miner ran through the tunnels to stay in shape.

Fortunately, after 17 days of isolation, rescuers discovered the miners and set up a supply line to provide them with food, water and nutritional supplements such as vitamin D to replace the nutrients they weren't getting from sunlight. Even socks, electric cables and inflatable beds were sent down the supply line.

On the surface, experts played an important role in the miners' survival. Psychologists and doctors were brought into the camp to keep the miners healthy but also busy and mentally focused. Submarine experts from the Chilean Navy worked closely with experts from NASA to share their experience on how to keep the miners in sound body and mind while trapped in such remote, small quarters.

The rescue was achieved by drilling a 624-meter shaft beneath the ground and then lowering a rescue capsule to bring the miners up from the tunnel one by one. The rescuers didn't have the technology to rescue the miners, so the Chilean Navy designed the capsule "Phoenix." It took approximately 15 minutes to bring each of the men up. While each miner was riding up to the surface, his family was waiting anxiously above the mine. Many of them had been camping near the mine since the collapse.

## Grammar

**1** Read sentences 1–4 from the article. Look at the verbs in bold. Which describe a) a completed action? b) an action in progress at a point in the past?

1 The eyes of the world **were watching** as the capsule brought up the last of the 33 miners.
2 The men **had survived underground** for 69 days.
3 He **had been working** as a miner for 31 years before he became famous.
4 It **took** approximately 15 minutes to bring each of the men up.

**2** Complete 1–4 in the Grammar panel with the correct tense. Then complete a–d with sentences 1–4 in 1.

**3** **a** Complete the text with a past form of the verbs in parentheses.

Daniel Defoe (1) .................... *(wrote)* *Robinson Crusoe* after he (2) .................... *(read)* about a real sailor on a desert island: Alexander Selkirk. In 1705, Selkirk (3) .................... *(work)* on a ship when he suddenly (4) .................... *(demand)* to be left on a remote island off the coast of Chile. While he (5) .................... *(sail)* on the ship, he (6) .................... *(realize)* that the captain was incapable of controlling it. He (7) .................... *(learn)* a number of skills in previous jobs that (8) .................... *(help)* him to survive on the island. When he was finally rescued, Selkirk (9) .................... *(live)* on the island for four years. Afterward, he (10) .................... *(go)* back to sea and eventually he (11) .................... *(die)* of yellow fever while he (12) .................... *(travel)* around the coast of Africa.

**b** 3.3 Listen and compare your answers. Are they the same? If not, are your answers also possible?

**4** **a** Complete the sentences so they are true for you.

1 Before I was 12, I'd never...
2 I was... last week when...
3 I'd been... for years when I...
4 When I heard about... I was...

**b** Compare your sentences with a partner's. Are any of them similar?

### Narrative Tenses

**Past simple & past continuous**

We use the (1) .................... to talk about actions completed at a specific point in the past. These tell the main events in a story in the order they happened:
(a) ....................

We use the (2) ....................

1 for an action in progress at a point in the past:
(b) ....................

2 to talk about simultaneous actions in the past:
*While each miner was traveling up to the surface, their families were waiting anxiously.*

**Past perfect & past perfect continuous**

We use the (3) .................... to talk about an event that happened before a point in the past:
(c) ....................

We use the (4) .................... to talk about a longer action in progress before another action in the past (often continuing up to this action):
(d) ....................

*See page 142 for grammar reference and more practice.*

## Speaking

**1** **a** Work in pairs. Act out an interview. Student A, you are a reporter from an overseas TV station. Student B, you are one of the rescued miners. Talk about...

- the moment of the accident
- day-to-day life in the tunnel
- the miners' feelings and concerns
- the leadership and encouragement from the shift leader
- staying mentally and physically fit
- the rescue and being reunited with family
- life and plans after the rescue.

**b** Switch roles and act out the interview again.

a

b

c

d

e

## SPEAKING & LISTENING

**1** Work in groups. Look at the images and answer the questions.

1 What are the people doing in each image? How do you think they feel?
2 Have you ever done any of these activities? If so, did you enjoy the experience? If not, would you like to? Why/Why not?
3 What is a "thrill seeker"? Are you one? Do you know anyone who is?

**2 a** 3.4 Listen to four people talking about extreme activities. Match speakers 1–4 to four of the images a–e.

**b** Mark the correct column(s) for speakers 1–4.

| | 1 | 2 | 3 | 4 |
|---|---|---|---|---|
| 1 Who is a thrill seeker? | | | | |
| 2 Who does the activity a lot? | | | | |
| 3 Who enjoys the activity? | | | | |
| 4 Who thinks the activity is frightening? | | | | |
| 5 Who needed training to do the activity? | | | | |

## VOCABULARY: Talking about danger

**1 a** Complete the extracts from Transcript 3.4 with the words in the box.

about (x2)   go   in (x2)   into   take   took

1 Lots of things could .................... **wrong**.
2 I don't **care** .................... the risks.
3 I don't want to put my life .................... **danger**.
4 The organization... .................... all the necessary **precautions**.
5 We got .................... **trouble** at one point.
6 They **warn** you .................... the sharks and their behavior.
7 You can't .................... **risks** with wild animals.
8 In the dive cage you can watch them .................... **safety**.

**b** Listen to 3.4 again and check.

**2 a** Fill in blanks 1–6 with the correct form of the phrases in bold in 1a.

Your friends want to go rock climbing. They tell you it's safe and nothing can (1) *go wrong*. You don't like (2) .................... ...................., and you've read a blog (3) .................... people .................... rock falls in the area. Some people got (4) .................... .................... last month, and a helicopter had to rescue them. Your friends don't (5) .................... .................... the risks and say the company will (6) .................... all the necessary .................... .

**b** Work in pairs. What would you do in this situation? Would you trust your friends or the Internet?

*If you're not an experienced rock climber, anything could go wrong!*

## Listening

**1 a** Work in pairs. You are going to listen to a psychologist discussing why people take risks. What do you think she might say about topics a–d?

a the link between excitement and adrenaline ..........
b teenage boys ..........
c modern life ..........
d genetics and evolution ..........

**b** 3.5 Listen and check your ideas in 1a. Number the topics in the order they are discussed.

**2** According to Dr. Aziz, what is the connection between...

1 horror movies and risk taking?
2 a risk taking gene and hunting large animals?
3 modern life and extreme sports?
4 testosterone and teenagers doing extreme sports?

**3** Work in pairs. Discuss the questions.

- Apart from extreme sports, in what other ways do people take risks in life?
- What's the biggest risk that you, or someone you know, has taken?
- "Only a person who risks is free" (unknown). Do you agree with this quote? Why/Why not?

## Grammar

**1** Read extracts a–d. Underline the adverbs.

a Let's examine these questions carefully.
b Much of modern life is extremely boring.
c He's always going rock climbing—I never see him on weekends!
d Obviously, teenage boys are the biggest thrill seekers of all.

**2 a** Read section A in the Grammar panel. Match sentences a–d in 1 to the four uses.

**b** Read section B in the Grammar panel. Choose the correct answer for 1–5.

**3 a** Write the adverb form of the word in parentheses in the correct place in each sentence.

1 I don't *usually* go on extreme rides at amusement parks. *(usual)*
2 I wouldn't go white-water rafting. It's too dangerous. *(person)*
3 I learn new sports, so I'd love to do a new hobby like ice climbing. *(quick)*
4 It's easy to see animals in the wild in my country. *(incredible)*
5 I play soccer, but I still love it. *(bad)*
6 Tourists come to my hometown to do extreme sports. *(often)*
7 I read the safety instructions before doing any activity that could be dangerous. *(careful)*

**b** Work in pairs. Are the sentences in 3a true for you?

### Adverbs

**A Uses**

1 We can use adverbs to add information to a verb:
- adverbs of manner say how we do something:
  *He spoke very quickly.*
- adverbs of frequency say how often we do something:
  *She often goes mountain biking on the weekend.*

2 We can also use adverbs to modify an adjective:
*Kite surfing can be incredibly dangerous.*

3 Sentence adverbs describe a whole sentence and often show the speaker's attitude to what is being said (e.g., *interestingly*, *honestly*):
*Honestly, I don't care what he does.*

**B Position of adverbs**

1 Adverbs of manner usually go at the (1)*beginning / end* of a clause or sentence.
2 Adverbs of frequency usually go:
(2)*before / after* the verb they describe.
(3)*before / after* the verb *to be* or other auxiliary verb.
3 Adverbs go (4)*before / after* the adjective they modify.
4 Sentence adverbs usually go at the (5)*beginning / end* of a sentence.

*See page 142 for grammar reference and more practice.*

**Notice** *extreme*

*Extreme* is increasingly used to describe new variations on traditional sports:
*extreme skiing, extreme cycling*
It is also used to describe crazy new sports like extreme ironing.
Is *extreme* used in the same way in your language?

## Speaking

**1 a** Work in groups. You have won a competition for an extreme weekend. Decide...

- what activity to do
- where/when you will do it
- what risks are involved
- what preparations you need to make (e.g., medical checkup, equipment).

**b** Present your ideas to the class. Which group has the most unusual/most dangerous idea?

a

b

c

## READING & VOCABULARY: Weather

**1** Work in groups. Answer the questions.

1 Look at the images. What weather conditions do they show? What do they have in common?
2 Do you have four seasons in your country? What is the weather usually like in each season?
3 How many weather words do you know? Make a list. Are the words nouns, verbs or adjectives?

**2** **a** Work in pairs. Student A, read story 1. Student B, read story 2. Which image a–d is each story about?

**b** Read your story again and answer the questions.

1 What was the first sign of bad weather?
2 What were the serious weather conditions?
3 Did the person stay in the car? Was this a good idea?
4 What other actions saved the person's life?

**3** Work in the same pairs as in 2a. Retell your story in your own words, using the questions in 2b as a guide.

**4** **a** Work in pairs. Use a dictionary if necessary. Find words in stories 1 and 2 that mean...

1 a thick cloud near ground level, reducing visibility ......*fog*......
2 small pieces of ice that fall from the sky like rain ............
3 a crashing sound during a storm ............
4 a severe snowstorm with strong winds ............
5 a bank of deep snow created by strong winds ............
6 a very powerful wind ............
7 a sudden flash of light during a storm ............
8 a rotating column of very strong wind. ............

**b** Answer the questions.

1 Which weather conditions occur a) in the Arctic Circle? b) during a tropical storm?
2 Which words are most useful to talk about the weather in your country?

# Survivors'

## 1 Snowed In

*It's been an unhappy New Year's Eve for the inhabitants of Sakhalin, Russia. Several motorists have been caught in their cars by a severe blizzard. Trapped by snowdrifts, some 50 people have needed help from emergency services. Sadly, several of the rescue workers are now also missing, and their current status is unknown.*

I heard this story on the news this evening. Something similar happened to me a few years ago while I was traveling in northern Finland. I had ignored warnings of freezing weather on the radio, and my car became trapped in a snowdrift. There was fog everywhere. It was freezing cold, and I was alone. Fortunately, I had my cell phone with me and was able to contact the emergency services for help.

I was told not to leave the car. To stay warm, I had to turn the motor on and off from time to time. It's dangerous to keep the motor running continuously as snow can block the air, trapping dangerous gases inside. I was also told to keep my arms and legs moving. That was difficult because I wasn't able to move a lot in the driver's seat. Nevertheless, there were some exercises that I could do like the leg movements that I'd learned for long-haul flights. In the end, I was rescued after three hours, and I can only hope that the people in Russia get the same quick assistance that I did.

# Tales

## 2 Tornado

While driving on the highway one day in 1999, Oklahoma resident Kevin Weber was caught in a sudden storm. As hailstones began hitting his car, he decided to park under a bridge for protection. What he didn't know was that he was about to get caught in the heart of a tornado that was moving rapidly across the Midwestern USA.

With the hailstones, rain was pouring from the sky. In those circumstances, Weber did what anyone would have done. As a tornado is often accompanied by thunder and flashes of lightning, most people try to wait underneath a bridge to survive the storm. However, that can be a deadly mistake.

When a gale blows under a bridge, it enters a narrow space. This forces the winds together, and they become even more powerful. Furthermore, other objects can be blown under the bridge by the wind and can cause serious injuries if they hit someone.

Luckily, Weber made a decision that saved his life. He left his car and lay flat on the ground. He watched as the tornado suddenly lifted up his vehicle and threw it out from under the bridge. As the storm slowly ended, Weber left to search for his car. Eventually, he found it a kilometer away, so damaged that it was almost unrecognizable. Although his car was a wreck, Weber had been fortunate. Tragically, many other people were killed in that powerful storm.

## Pronunciation: Sentence adverbs

**1 a** 3.6 Listen to these sentences from the stories. Notice how the speaker says the adverbs. Are they stressed or unstressed?

1 Sadly, several of the rescue workers are now missing.
2 Tragically, many other people were killed in that powerful storm.
3 Fortunately, I had my cell phone with me.
4 Luckily, Weber made a decision that saved his life.

**b** Listen again. How does the intonation on the adverbs emphasize the speaker's attitude?

**2** Practice reading the sentences in 1 with the correct stress and intonation.

**3 a** Complete the sentences with an appropriate sentence/attitude adverb.

1 ………………, we had good weather for the picinic.
2 The storm was terrible, but ……………… I had my umbrella with me.
3 ………………, they found one survivor after three days of rescue operations.
4 ... but ………………, there was nothing they could do to save any others.

**b** Practice reading out your sentences with the appropriate stress on the adverbs. How does your choice of adverb affect the way you read each sentence?

## Speaking & Writing

**1 a** Work in small groups. Discuss the questions. What is...

- the hottest weather you have experienced?
- the coldest you have ever been?
- the most unusual weather you have experienced?

**b** Tell the group about a bad weather experience you have had. What happened? What did you do? Did you make good or bad decisions?

**2** Work in pairs. Choose one of the experiences from 1b and write a short article about it. Include...

- what you were doing and where you were
- the weather conditions
- what actions you had to take as a result
- how this affected you
- the end result.

a

b

## TUNE IN

**1** Look at the images. Which activity would you prefer to do on vacation? Why?

**2** **a** 3.7 Listen to a conversation between Josh and Scott. What is the link between the conversation and the images?

**b** Listen again. Take notes on what the speakers say about each topic.

1 weather
2 clothes
3 first aid
4 driving
5 pickpockets
6 entertainment

## FOCUS ON LANGUAGE

**3** **a** Match 1–7 to a–g to complete the warnings.

1 **Remember to** pack
2 **You might want to** take
3 If you're taking new boots, **make sure**
4 **You want to be careful**
5 **I wouldn't** drive
6 **You don't want to**
7 **You definitely shouldn't**

a down the coastal highway if I were you.
b get stuck in a traffic jam.
c you use them a couple of times before you go.
d some good waterproof clothing.
e some Band-Aids in case you get blisters.
f take your car down there.
g on those little country roads.

**b** Listen to 3.7 again and check your answers.

**4** Work in pairs. Use the expressions in 3a to give a warning or piece of advice to someone who is going...

1 to the jungle.
2 to the desert.
3 long-distance sailing.
4 ice climbing.
5 to live abroad for a year.

### Warnings

3.8 Listen to the sentences and underline the stressed words. Does the intonation go up or down at the end?

1 You want to be careful on those little country roads.
2 You don't want to be stuck in a traffic jam.
3 You might want to take some Band-Aids.

Listen again and repeat with the correct stress and intonation.

## OVER TO YOU

**5** Work in pairs. What warnings would you give tourists visiting your country? Make a list.

**6** **a** Read the role cards and act out the situation.

**Student A**

A friend is planning to visit your country for two weeks and has called you to ask for advice. You want to be completely honest but also give positive and realistic recommendations.

**Student B**

You are visiting a friend in another country for two weeks. Call him/her to ask about: the weather, the food, health issues, safety, places to visit and whether people speak English.

**b** Switch roles and act out the situation again.

## TUNE IN

**1** Work in pairs. Look at the images and answer the questions.

1 How are the people feeling? Why?
2 Have you ever been in a similar situation? If so, where were you?

**2 a** 3.9 Ayaka has moved to New York from Japan. Listen to her talking to a friend. Which image shows Ayaka?

a b

**b** Listen again and answer the questions.

1 What problem does Ayaka have?
2 What has she done to try and solve it?
3 Has she been successful? Why/Why not?
4 What positive experience has she had?
5 What is Laura's attitude to Ayaka? How do you know?

## PREPARE FOR TASK

**3 a** Complete sentences 1–8 with the words in the box.

always better completely hard must poor sorry sounds

1 I'm .................... to hear that.
2 That must be really .................... .
3 That .................... really difficult.
4 You .................... feel terrible.
5 You .................... thing.
6 Things will get .................... soon.
7 I .................... understand.
8 I'm .................... here for you.

**b** Check your answers in Transcript 3.9 on page 162.

**4** Underline three expressions in the transcript that Ayaka uses to introduce her problems.

**5** Work in pairs. Read the e-mail and answer the questions.

1 What country is Naomi in? What's she doing there?
2 What problems is she having? Make a list.
3 What advice would you give her? Think of two ideas for each problem.

Hey Naomi,

Thanks for the e-mail. Sorry to hear you're finding it difficult to get settled in Berlin. The weather can't help! Minus two degrees sounds very cold—brrrrr! I won't tell you about my day at the beach!

I know it's tough making friends in another country, but now you've started classes at the university, I'm sure you'll meet lots of people. And I'm sure your German's better than you think! Anyway, it's going to improve really quickly now that you're living there!

Are you still staying with that family? It can't be easy living in such a noisy house—you need somewhere quiet for studying! And the food they give you sounds horrible! Everything seems so expensive there as well—what are you going to do?

Anyway, can't wait to come and visit! Jason

## TASK

**6 a** Work in pairs. Act out a conversation between Naomi and a friend who is visiting her in Berlin.

**Student A**

You are Naomi. Tell your friend about the problems you are having. Use the expressions in 4.

**Student B**

You are Naomi's friend. Listen to her problems and be as supportive as possible. Use the expressions in 3a.

**b** Switch roles and act out the conversation again.

## REPORT BACK

**7** Tell the class who was the more supportive and sympathetic friend, A or B. Why? Who gave better advice?

→ Go to Review A, Unit 3, p. 36 → Go to Writing Bank 2, p. 153

# VOCABULARY

## People you know

**1** Work in pairs. Which of these people do you know? When/Where do you usually see them? Add three more relationship nouns to the list.

acquaintance close friend coworker roommate parents-in-law manager teammate

**2** R1 Listen to four short extracts. Which speaker 1–4 is talking about...

a an acquaintance? c a partner?
b classmates? d coworkers?

## Phrasal verbs

**3** R2 Complete the extracts from the audio with a verb. Then listen and check.

1 We usually .................... up in a café when we finish work on Fridays. It's a great place to .................... out.
2 I .................... up Chinese last year. I often .................... up late and miss something important.
3 We argue a lot, but we always .................... up afterward. Most of the time we .................... along well.
4 We were at college together, but she .................... out after a few months. We .................... into each other all the time.

**4** Work in pairs. Complete the sentences so they are true for you.

1 I'd really like to take up...
2 Someone I really don't get along with is...
3 When I was fourteen, I always hung out...

# GRAMMAR

## Auxiliary verbs

**1 a** Complete the conversation with the correct form of an auxiliary verb. Leave two blanks empty.

**A** .................... the Wildcats win the game last night?
**B** No, they .................... . They .................... playing very well at the moment!
**A** So who .................... won?
**B** The Dayton Jets.
**A** Oh, well. They're the best team in the league, .................... they?
**B** They're good, but I really .................... think we can win the championship this year.
**A** Really? What .................... makes you think that?
**B** The new power forward, Natalia Vicente. She's the best player I .................... ever seen!

**b** Work in pairs. Invent a similar conversation about a sports team you support.

## Past participles

**2 a** Find and correct five mistakes in the words in bold.

Yesterday, I (1)**was send** a strange e-mail. It was from my friend Esther. It said: "I (2)**'ve been involved** in a robbery during a trip to London. I (3)**'ve have** my money and credit card (4)**stolen**." She then asked for $2,000 to (5)**be transfer to** a bank account. However, I know she (6)**hasn't visited** London for years so it must be a hacker. I (7)**'ve contact** her at a different address to let her know what (8)**'s happened**. Make sure you have (9)**update** firewall software to prevent this happening to you!

**b** Work in pairs. Have you, or has anyone you know, been sent an e-mail like this? What did it say? What did you/they do?

## Reflexive pronouns

**3** Work in pairs. Make true sentences about you, your friends or family using the verbs and reflexive pronouns.

1 blame myself 3 hurt himself/herself
2 enjoy ourselves 4 express themselves

*My friends and I enjoy ourselves most at parties.*

# FUNCTIONAL LANGUAGE

## Small talk

**1 a** Choose the correct option to complete each sentence.

1 I'm not really a big fan *for / of* spicy food to be honest.
2 *Speak / Speaking* of music, there's a festival here on the weekend.
3 I see you've *brought / taken* the wet weather with you!
4 I have a leaflet in my bag with recommendations for places to visit. *Do / Would* you like to see it?
5 I went on a school trip to your city *once / one time*.

**b** Work in pairs. Choose a sentence in 1a. Use it to begin a conversation with your partner. How long can you keep the conversation going?

## LOOKING BACK

- Write down three new irregular past participles that you have learned in this unit.
- Is there anything in this unit you want to look at again?
- Choose one reading text from the unit. What new information did you learn from it?

## VOCABULARY

### Medical experts

**1 a** Work in pairs. Name two people who...

1 work in a hospital.
2 practice alternative/complementary medicine.
3 use natural remedies.

**b** Which medical experts have you found most helpful? Which would you never visit? Why?

### Symptoms & treatment

**2** Match the words in the box to the images.

antibiotics backache bandage bruise
cough syrup bump Band-Aid rash

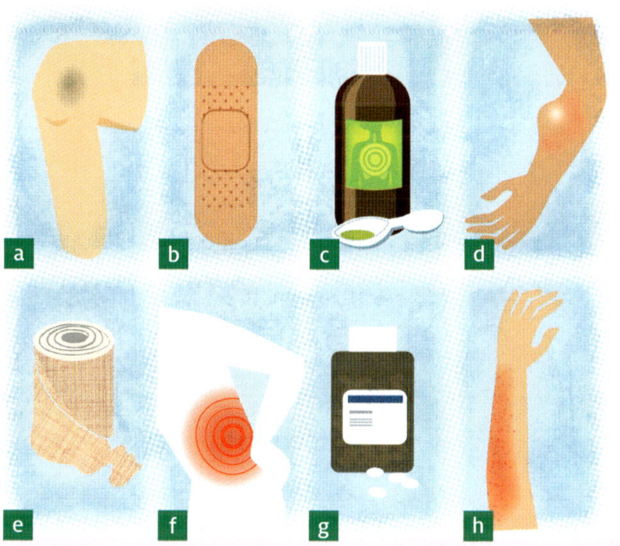


**3** Work in pairs. Discuss the questions.

- What do you usually take if you get a cold?
- Do you always make an appointment to see the doctor when you feel sick? Why/Why not?
- Have you ever needed a vaccination to travel somewhere?

### *-ever*

**4 a** Choose the correct option to complete the sentences.

1 *However* / *Whenever* I go to a party, I try to look nice.
2 I'd never give away confidential information, *whoever* / *whatever* asked me!
3 *Whatever* / *Whichever* you do in my country, don't drive on the wrong side of the street!
4 *However many* / *However much* times I watch Charlie Chaplin movies, they always make me laugh.

**b** Work in pairs. Change the underlined information in 4a so the sentences are true for you.

## GRAMMAR

### The present

**1** Complete the sentences with the best form of the verbs in parentheses. Then ask and answer the questions in pairs.

1 What .......... you usually .......... in your free time? *(do)*
2 What .......... you .......... at the moment? *(read)*
3 How long .......... you .......... in this city? *(live)*
4 What time .......... your English class .......... today? *(finish)*
5 .......... you .......... any good movies recently? *(see)*

### *Used to do/Used to doing*

**2** Work in pairs. Complete the sentences so they are true for you.

1 When I was a kid, I used to .......... .
2 In my family we're not used to .......... .
3 When they were young, my grandparents weren't used to .......... .
4 I didn't get used to .......... until I graduated.
5 Now that I have a .........., I'm getting used to .......... .

## FUNCTIONAL LANGUAGE

### Making polite requests

**1 a** Complete the sentences with the words in the box.

can could do idea mind
possible tell wonder would (x2)

1 .......... you .......... lending me your cell phone?
2 .......... you have any .......... where the nearest post office is?
3 I .......... if you .......... recommend something for insomnia.
4 .......... you .......... me what time the supermarket closes?
5 .......... it be .......... to give me a lift to the bus stop after class?

**b** R3 Listen and check.

**2** Work in pairs. Take turns asking the questions in 1a and giving an appropriate answer.

### LOOKING BACK

- Which lesson in this unit did you enjoy most? Why?
- Think of five useful expressions from this unit and when you might use them.
- Tell your partner about something you have done recently that has had a good or bad effect on you.

# VOCABULARY

## Equipment

**1** Work in pairs. Which of the items in the box have you used? What did you use them for?

binoculars compass first-aid kit flashlight life jacket ropes waterproof clothing

## Personality adjectives

**2 a** Complete the sentences with your own ideas. Then compare your ideas in groups.

1 I think it's *reckless* and *irresponsible* to... because...
2 The most *courageous* person I know is... because...
3 You need to be very *experienced* in... if you want to...
4 You'd need to be *resourceful* and *self-sufficient* to be able to... because...

**b** Use two of the words in *italics* in 2a to describe people you know. Give reasons for your answers.

## Talking about danger

**3 a** Complete the text with the words in the box.

danger precautions risks safely trouble wrong

When you do extreme sports, things can easily go (1) ........................ . For this reason, it's important to take the necessary (2) ........................ . When I went white-water rafting, we had to wear life jackets and helmets so we could go down the river (3) ........................ . We were also given instructions about what to do if we got into (4) ........................ and fell out of the raft. You will only be in (5) ........................ if you take unnecessary (6) ........................ .

**b** Work in pairs. Think of another extreme sport. What could go wrong? What precautions should you take?

# GRAMMAR

## Narrative tenses

**1 a** Complete the sentences with the correct form of the verbs in parentheses.

1 When I was ten, my family and I ........................ *(go)* to **Italy** on vacation.
2 I ........................ *(run into)* **an old school friend** while I ........................ *(shop)* **yesterday**.
3 Before I was ten, I ........................ *(never travel)* **abroad**.
4 I ........................ *(learn)* **karate** for months when I ........................ *(decide)* to **take up tai chi**.
5 By the time I ........................ *(arrive)* at **the concert**, **the band** ........................ *(play)* for **an hour**.

**b** Work in pairs. Change the information in bold in 1a so the sentences are true for you.

## Adverbs

**2 a** Choose the adverb that reflects your opinion and write it in the correct position in the sentence.

1 I go surfing in the summer. *never / sometimes / often*
2 I always read safety instructions. *carefully / quickly*
3 Rock climbing is dangerous. *extremely / fairly*
4 We've had a very hot summer this year. *luckily / unfortunately*

**b** Work in pairs. Use the adverb form of the words in the box to make true sentences about yourself or people you know.

bad fortune incredible usual worrying

*I don't usually go out on Sunday nights.*

# FUNCTIONAL LANGUAGE

## Giving warnings

**1 a** R4 Listen and match warnings 1–6 to images a–c.

**b** Complete the warnings. Then listen again and check.

1 You ........................ ........................ to wear a wetsuit to protect you from the cold.
2 You ........................ ........................ go too fast or it might be difficult to stop.
3 You ........................ to be careful if the waves ........................ really big.
4 When you buy sneakers, ........................ ........................ they're half a size bigger than your regular size.
5 You ........................ want to ........................ stuck up a mountain in the middle of a blizzard.
6 I ........................ ........................ old shoes as this can cause injuries.

**2** Work in pairs. Give two more warnings for each activity in the images.

## LOOKING BACK

- Which story from this unit impressed you most? Why?
- How many adverbs can you remember from the unit?
- Think of a time when the weather affected your plans. What happened? Tell your partner.

## READING

**1** Work in pairs. Look at the image of Etienne, an English student. What do you think his problem is?

**2 a** Read Etienne's blog post and check your ideas in 1. Summarize his problem in one sentence.

When I started learning English, I felt I made so much progress each day. I went from elementary to intermediate level in just two years. But recently I'm making much slower progress—I haven't improved at all, or at least that's how it feels. I *am* proud of my level, but I'd hoped to be in an advanced class by now. I realize I need to improve my listening and accuracy, but because I can already use English well enough, I don't have the same need to study as I used to. Does anyone have any tips for getting past this stage?

**b** Work in pairs. Compare your summary sentences. What level do you think Etienne is? Do you ever feel like this?

**3** Work in groups. Discuss what advice you would give Etienne.

**4 a** Read the comments from two of Etienne's classmates. Do they give any of the advice you discussed in 3?

**b** R5 Read again and choose the correct option to complete the texts. Then listen and check.

**Monika** I'm sorry to (1) *know / hear* you're feeling down, Eti. I think the key is to be more (2) *self-sufficient / self-conscious*. You could (3) *ever / always* sign up for a news website with audio podcasts. This is a great way to improve your listening skills. You (4) *might / could* want to get a conversation exchange partner, too. (5) *Whatever / However* you do, don't get demotivated. Don't just study English... live it!

**Sachiko** I'm (6) *playing / always playing* video games when I should be studying English! It was the same when I (7) *studied / was studying* for my exams. Then my father gave me a study planner and suggested I "block out" times for studying. For example, I (8) *spend / 'm spending* 30 minutes Skyping a friend in the States every Friday morning. I set (9) *me / myself* little goals at the beginning of each week, like "I'm going to learn ten words about architecture." Then, at the end of the week, I can say I (10) *'ve improved / improved*.

## SPEAKING

**5** Work in groups. Discuss the questions.

- Who do you think gave Etienne the best advice? Why?
- Would you follow any of the advice yourself? Why/Why not?
- What areas of your English do you feel you need to work on most? Give each other suggestions on how to do this.

**6 a** Make a study diary for one week, with blocks of time marked for English practice. Decide a) what you are going to do, b) when and c) for how long.

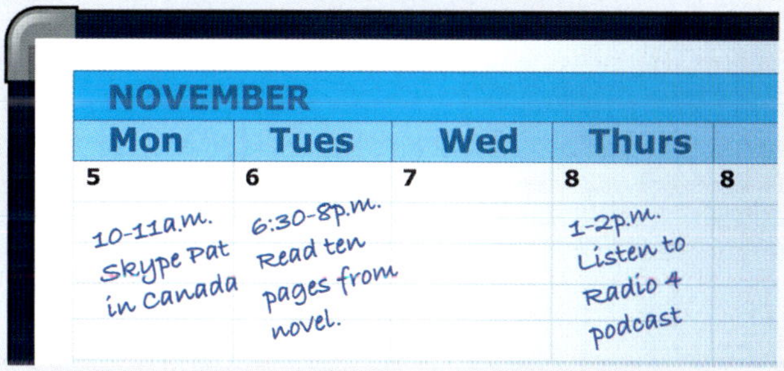


**b** Work in pairs. Compare your diaries. Does your partner have any ideas that you would like to add to yours?

**7** Follow your day planner for one week. Then discuss the questions in small groups.

- Did you stick to your plan? If not, what happened?
- Did it help you feel that your English was improving?

## QUICK CHECK

Complete the checklist below.

| Can you... | Yes, I can. | Yes, more or less. | I need to look again. |
|---|---|---|---|
| 1 talk about different relationships? | ☐ | ☐ | ☐ |
| 2 make small talk? | ☐ | ☐ | ☐ |
| 3 discuss problems and find solutions? | ☐ | ☐ | ☐ |
| 4 talk about health and fitness? | ☐ | ☐ | ☐ |
| 5 make polite requests? | ☐ | ☐ | ☐ |
| 6 discuss survival stories? | ☐ | ☐ | ☐ |
| 7 talk about extreme weather conditions? | ☐ | ☐ | ☐ |
| 8 give warnings? | ☐ | ☐ | ☐ |

Compare your answers with a partner's.

- What else do you know now after studying units 1–3?
- Do you need to look again at any of the sections?

# 4 REINVENTION

a

b

**1** Work in pairs. Look at the images and answer the questions.

1 What do the images show? What is the connection between the images and the title of the unit?
2 How have the people changed their appearance?
3 Why do you think they have done this?
4 What else do people do to change their appearance?

**2** **a** 4.1 Listen to an interview with an image consultant talking about a band. Match band members 1–3 to the looks in images a–c.

1 the drummer
2 the singer
3 the guitarist

**b** Listen again. How is each band member going to change his/her look?

**3** Work in pairs. Complete A in the KEY VOCABULARY PANEL. Which words can you match to the images?

**4** **a** Complete the extracts with words from A in the KEY VOCABULARY PANEL.

1 His face and body are covered in beautiful tribal .......................... .
2 It's also common in Polynesia to get a .......................... like this red one in his ear.
3 He's going to grow a .......................... and a .......................... .
4 Goths put on white makeup so they look very .......................... .
5 The contrast of the girl's black and .......................... blue hair looks amazing.
6 I love the straight .......................... —it's a really impressive look.

**b** 4.2 Listen and check.

a

b

c

d

*Appetizers: .............. , ....................*

*Main course: ....................*

*Dessert: ....................*

*Drink: ....................*

## TUNE IN

**1** Work in pairs. Discuss the questions.

- What dishes do the photos show? Have you tried any of them? Which ones? If not, would you like to?
- What country do you think they're from?
- How would you describe the dishes? Talk about the ingredients, flavors and textures.

**2 a** 5.9 Listen to a conversation and answer the questions.

1 Where are the speakers?
2 What country are they in?
3 Which of the dishes in the images do they mention?

**b** Listen again. Write the names of the dishes in the box in the correct section of the menu above.

golabki makowiec barszcz kawa zurek

**3 a** Take notes on the ingredients and flavor for each dish in 2b.

**b** Compare your notes with a partner's. Then listen again to check or add details.

## PREPARE FOR TASK

**4 a** Choose the correct option. Check your answers in Transcript 5.9 on page 158.

1 Typical *dishes / plates* use lots of cabbage, meat and sour cream.
2 I *recommend you / 'd recommend* the barszcz.
3 What *does it taste like / taste does it have*?
4 ... and vinegar, which *gives / makes* it a sour flavor.
5 It *serves / comes* with a boiled egg in it.
6 It's usually *serve / served* in a bowl made of traditional Polish bread.
7 *It takes / It's* a long time to prepare!
8 What's it made *with / of*?

**b** Which sentences from 4a describe these dishes?

- barszcz
- zurek
- golabki
- makowiec

**5** Describe the dishes in images a–d. Use the expressions in 4a.

*It has honey in it, which gives it a lovely sweet flavor.*

## TASK

**6** Design a three-course meal using typical food from your country. Choose an appetizer, a main course and a dessert. Prepare notes on

- the ingredients and flavors
- how the dishes are prepared and served.

**7 a** Act out the situation in pairs. Use the expressions in 4a.

**Student A**

You are with a foreign visitor in a restaurant in your country. Suggest the three-course meal you designed in **6**.

**Student B**

You are visiting another country. You are having dinner in a restaurant with your host. Listen to his/her suggestions for which dishes to choose. Ask and answer questions to find out more about each dish.

**b** Switch roles and act out the situation again.

## REPORT BACK

**8** Tell the class about your partner's most interesting dish. Why did you like it? Which dish would you most like to try as a class?

➜ Go to Review B, Unit 5, p. 69 ➜ Go to Writing Bank 3, p. 154

# 6 THAT'S ENTERTAINMENT

e

**1** Work in pairs. Look at the images and answer the questions.

1. What kinds of entertainment do they show? Which ones are popular in your country?
2. Which ones have you seen? Which do you like/dislike? Why?
3. What's your favorite kind of entertainment? Why?

**2** Work in pairs. Complete A in the KEY VOCABULARY PANEL. Use a dictionary to help you.

f

**3** **a** 6.1 Listen and number the images 1–6 in the order you hear them.

**b** Listen again and answer the questions.

1 What kind of street performers does Karen mention?
2 Why does Kinuko dislike circuses?
3 Why are the *Hun Lakhon Lek* puppeteers so elegant?
4 Why does Vishal like Tarantino movies?
5 What warning does Julie give about stand-up comedy shows?
6 Why does Helmut prefer the theater to the movies?

**4** Work in pairs. Complete B and C in the KEY VOCABULARY PANEL. Use a dictionary to help you.

**NOTICE** ENTERTAINMENT VERBS
We say:
*make/shoot a movie* BUT *put on/perform a play*

**5** Work in groups. What did you like/dislike about the last piece of entertainment you saw? Talk about some of these things.

- atmosphere
- cast
- characters
- plot
- performances
- scenery
- special effects
- music/soundtrack
- the ending

*I saw a dance show last week. It was hilarious and completely unpredictable. The cast…*

## KEY VOCABULARY

### Entertainment

### A People in entertainment

- Which of the words in the box can you find in the images?

audience circus performer magician makeup artist
mime artist puppet/puppeteer scriptwriter
sound engineer stand-up comedian street performer

- Which people…
  1 are entertainers?
  2 work behind the scenes?
  3 watch entertainment?

### B Movies & theater

- Complete sentences 1–10 with the words in the box.

cast part performance plot scene scenery
script soundtrack special effects stage

1 Quentin Tarantino wrote the .................... for *Reservoir Dogs* in three weeks.
2 I didn't understand the movie because the .................... was so complicated.
3 The actors gave their best .................... of the show so far.
4 John Williams has composed the music for the .................... of this movie and many others.
5 The balcony .................... in *Romeo and Juliet* is very famous.
6 Movie studios now use computers to create many .................... .
7 We have front row seats—right next to the .................... !
8 I'd love to play the .................... of Sophie in *Mamma Mia*.
9 *Vicky Cristina Barcelona* has a great .................... —the three leading actors are excellent!
10 She's a talented artist and paints the .................... for many shows.

- Which words are related to a) movies? b) theater? c) both?

### C Entertainment adjectives

- Mark the adjectives in the box that the speakers in the audio used. What were they describing? Check your answers in Transcript 6.1 on page 158.

| | | | | | |
|---|---|---|---|---|---|
| action-packed | ........ | depressing | ........ | gripping | ........ |
| hilarious | ........ | intriguing | ........ | memorable | ........ |
| moving | ........ | predictable | ........ | | |
| (un)realistic | ........ | uplifting | ........ | | |

- Are the adjectives positive (+) or negative (–)? Which adjectives describe entertainment you have seen recently?

■ PRACTICE THE PASSIVE VOICE
■ TALK ABOUT MOVIES & REMAKES

## SPEAKING & READING

**1** Work in pairs. Answer the questions.

1 What do the images show? What is happening in each scene?
2 What kind of movie does each image show?
3 What kinds of movie do you prefer? Why?

**2** **a** Read the article from a movie magazine. Answer the questions.

1 What are the names of the movies in the images?
2 What is a "remake"?

a

**b** Read the article again. Complete the chart with information about the two movies.

| | *Yojimbo* | *A Fistful of Dollars* |
|---|---|---|
| 1 Director | | |
| 2 Lead actor | | |
| 3 Release date | | |
| 4 Setting (date/place) | | |

**3** Answer the questions about the article.

1 Why are remakes popular with moviemakers?
2 What are the similarities/differences between the two movies?
3 What was the reaction of critics to the remake?
4 Why did Kurosawa sue the makers of *A Fistful of Dollars*?

**4** Have you seen any remakes? Did you see the original version? Which version was better in your opinion?

b

# *Why make* A REMAKE?

Successful movies have been remade by Hollywood studios almost since the industry began. It is widely believed that a remake is a safe option for a moviemaker. Since the original version is already known to large numbers of people, a remake is much easier to sell to the public. This is no small thing when marketing a movie can be almost as expensive as making it.

One of the most successful remakes was the spaghetti western *A Fistful of Dollars*, a remake of the Japanese movie *Yojimbo*. It has often been said that both films are all-time classics of the adventure and western genres. *Yojimbo* (1961) was directed by Akiro Kurosawa and is considered to be one of the greatest movies ever made. It is often described as a comedy, though "satire" is perhaps a better word to use. The plot centers on the main character, a Samurai, played by Toshiro Mifune. He arrives in a Japanese village in the 1860s and soon gets caught in a war between two criminal gangs. Although he appears as a villain at the beginning of the movie, by the end he has become a hero by saving an innocent family from violence.

In 1964, *Yojimbo* was remade by Sergio Leone as *A Fistful of Dollars*. Unlike *Yojimbo*, the overall mood of this movie is more serious. It is set in the Old West, nineteenth-century Mexico, although it was filmed in Spain. An unknown American actor, Clint Eastwood, was chosen for the lead role. His character, like Yojimbo, is a loner who fights bandits, even though he seems just as cruel and violent as them, since he kills his enemies in a series of gunfights. However, Eastwood's character always spares innocent lives and shows that he too is a man of honor.

*A Fistful of Dollars* was a big hit in the USA. Leone's unique style of cinematography was widely acclaimed by critics. The acting, on the other hand, generally received bad reviews. Interestingly, Sergio Leone was never actually given permission to remake *Yojimbo*. Shortly after *A Fistful of Dollars* was released in Europe, Kurosawa sued the movie studio. As a result, he received 15% of the movie's profits. To this day, the connection to Kurosawa's movie is never mentioned in publicity.

## Grammar

**1** **a** Complete the sentences with the verbs in the box. Don't refer back to the article.

believed chosen filmed remade set

It is widely (1) .................. that a remake is a safe option for a moviemaker. *Yojimbo* was (2) .................. by Sergio Leone as *A Fistful of Dollars*. It is (3) .................. in the Old West, nineteenth-century Mexico, although it was (4) .................. in Spain. An unknown American actor, Clint Eastwood, was (5) .................. for the lead role.

**b** Check your answers in the article.

**2** **a** Look at the sentences in 1a and answer the questions.

1 Which sentence tells us exactly who is responsible for the action?
2 Why is it not necessary to name the people in the other sentences?
3 Which verb expresses an opinion? Whose opinion is it?

**b** Complete 1–3 in the Grammar panel with examples from 1a.

### The Passive Voice

**A With or without *by***

We use *by* to emphasize the person or thing responsible for the action:

(1) ..................................................

We don't use *by* when...

a) it's obvious who or what is responsible so we don't need to say.

b) we don't know who or what is responsible so we can't say:

(2) ..................................................

**B With reporting verbs**

We use the passive voice with reporting verbs (*say, think, believe*, etc.) to express other people's opinions without saying exactly whose opinions they are:

(3) ..................................................

*See page 145 for grammar reference and more practice.*

**3** **a** Report these opinions using the passive voice and the verbs in bold.

1 Some people **say** that movies are the highest form of art.
2 Many critics **believe** that computer games will have an enormous influence on movies in the future.
3 Many movie fans **claim** that modern moviemakers are obsessed with computer-generated effects.

**b** Work in pairs. Do you agree with the opinions in 3a? Why/Why not?

**4** **a** Read the movie review. Rewrite the underlined phrases using the passive voice. Only use *by* where you think it is important to say who or what is responsible.

(1)People believe that remakes are usually worse than the original version. One exception must be the 2010 Hollywood hit *The Tourist*, (2)which producers adapted from a little-known French film, *Anthony Zimmer*. The movie is about a criminal (3)who a mysterious woman (Angelina Jolie) is chasing for tax evasion. Johnny Depp plays a tourist who the police mistake for the criminal while on vacation in Venice.

(4)The screenwriter filled the script with surprises and action. (5)German moviemaker Florian Henckel von Donnersmarck directed it. (6)Critics nominated it for three Golden Globes, although (7)people think that it failed to win because audiences couldn't decide whether it was a thriller or a comedy, just like the original. (8)People have also said that the two main stars did not get along well during filming.

**b** Have you seen this movie? If so, what did you think of it? If not, would you like to?

### Notice — Adding information

In written texts it is common to use the passive voice after an active sentence. This allows us to add to the information at the end of the previous sentence:

*George Clooney is working on **a new movie. It is being filmed** in North Africa.*

## Speaking

**1** Work in groups. Discuss the questions.

- How do you prefer to watch movies? Do you rent them, download them or go to the movies?
- What differences are there when you watch movies through different media?
- Do you think going to the movies will eventually die out? Why/Why not?

a

b

c

## SPEAKING & LISTENING

**1** Work in groups. Discuss the questions.

1 What are the most popular hobbies in your country?
2 Think of an example of a hobby that is...
- dangerous
- expensive
- healthy
- unusual
- more popular with older people
- more popular with younger people.

3 Do you have a hobby? If so, how often do you do it? If not, is there anything you would like to take up?

**2** **a** Look at images a–d. What do they show? What countries are the activities associated with? How difficult do you think these activities are?

**b** 6.2 Listen to a radio show about unusual hobbies. Which two images do they talk about? Check your answers to 2a.

**3** **a** Listen again. Answer the questions about Miquela and Daniel.

1 When did he/she take up his/her hobby? Why?
2 When and where did the tradition start?

**b** What do the two hobbies have in common?

**4** Complete sentences 1–10 using your own words. Then listen again and check.

1 A *casteller* is...
2 ... are not very common but...
3 The bottom layer of the tower is made up of... because...
4 The upper layers are built as quickly as possible so...
5 The people at the top are... because...
6 A didgeridoo is...
7 99.9% of didgeridoos...
8 It's believed that if a didgeridoo is made by... it has...
9 You play the instrument by...
10 A common mistake made by students is...

**5** Work in pairs. Answer the questions.

1 Which of the activities in the audio would you like to see most? Why?
2 What activities are there in your country that have a cultural heritage?

## GRAMMAR

**1** **a** Work in pairs. What is the difference between sentences 1 and 2? Who took the photo in each case?

1 We took a photo.
2 We had a photo taken.

**b** Read the sentences. In which one did the speaker ask someone to make the instrument for him?

1 I had my didgeridoo made for me by an Australian Aboriginal.
2 My didgeridoo was made by an Australian Aboriginal.

**2** Read the GRAMMAR PANEL and complete 1–3 using the words in the box.

| ask get past participle |
|---|

**3** **a** Rewrite the sentences using *have* + object + past participle.

1 The gardener cut the grass last week.
*I had the grass cut last week.*
2 An optician has never checked my eyes. *I've...*
3 Decorators have been painting our house this week. *We've...*
4 I'm taking my car to the garage to be serviced tomorrow. *I'm...*

**b** Are any of the sentences in 3a true for anyone in the class? Change the time expressions if necessary.

d

**4** Work in pairs. Answer the questions.

1 Which of these things do you do yourself? Which do you have done by other people?
- cut hair
- print photos
- cook meals
- wash clothes
- fix the car/computer when it breaks down

2 What other things do you have done by other people? When was the last time you got them done? Who did them for you?
*I get my hair dyed every three months...*

3 Have you ever had anything stolen? If so, what? How did it happen?

### Have Something Done

We use *have* + object + (1) .................... to describe...

a) an action that we (2) .................... another person to do for us:
*We had our photo taken.*

b) a bad experience that happens to us:
*I had my credit card stolen.*

We can also use (3) .................... instead of *have*. It is common in informal, spoken English:
*I had/got my didgeridoo made especially for me.*

*See page 145 for grammar reference and more practice.*

## Vocabulary: Noun building suffixes

**1** **a** Look the sentences from Transcript 6.2. What is the root word of each word in bold?

1 All through my **childhood** I wanted to be one too.
2 There's only been one **fatality** in the last 30 years.
3 You can't show any **weakness**.
4 You can really feel the **tension** and **excitement**.

**b** Write the words from 1a in the chart.

| Suffix | Examples |
|---|---|
| 1 -sion | decision, .................... |
| 2 -hood | neighborhood, .................... |
| 3 -ity | creativity, .................... |
| 4 -ment | arrangement, .................... |
| 5 -ness | happiness, .................... |

**2** What nouns can you make by adding a suffix to the root words in the box? Add them to the chart in 1b.

mother  confuse  curious  entertain  lonely

**3** Choose five words from 1 or 2 and write sentences with blanks using them. Give your sentences to a partner to complete.
*I didn't have a very happy .................... . (child)*

## Pronunciation: Word stress

**1** **a** Match the words to the correct stress pattern according to the main stress and number of syllables.

oOo  Ooo  ooOoo

1 creativity ooOoo  3 decision ..........  5 loneliness ..........
2 curiosity ..........  4 excitement ..........  6 neighborhood ..........

**b** 6.3 Listen and check.

**2** 6.4 Match these words to the correct stress pattern in 1. Practice saying the words. Then listen and check.

flexibility  government  happiness  parenthood  revision

## Speaking

**1** **a** Work in groups of three. You want to start a new hobby together.

1 Each person choose a hobby (a different one for each group member).
2 Prepare notes about why it's a good hobby to take up.
3 Present the advantages of your hobby to the group.

**b** Discuss the advantages and disadvantages of each hobby until you reach an agreement on which one to do.

# 6.3 GAME ON!

■ DISCUSS COMPUTER GAMES

## SPEAKING

**1** Work in groups. Discuss the questions.

- What kinds of games can you see in the images?
- What other computer games are popular? Why do you think these games are so popular?
- Do you play computer games? If so, which ones? Where/When do you play them? Do you play on your own or with friends? If not, why?

a

b

## VOCABULARY: Computer games

**1** Work in pairs. Student A, complete text A with the words in the box. Student B, complete text B.

Text A Tomb Raider

first person go up a level graphics stages platform shoot 'em up

**Tomb Raider** is a (1) .................. game: you play the main character, Lara Croft. It's famous for its amazing (2) .................., and later versions of the game look like a movie. It's a (3) .................. game because you use your gun a lot against your enemies. But you need to use your head, too, if you want to move forward and (4) ................... It's also a (5) .................. game: you move through different (6) .................. until you reach the end.

Text B Wii Sports

console controller gameplay read motion sensor split screen

**Wii Sports** was the first big success for Nintendo's Wii (1) ................... With the (2) .................. in your hand, you can play several different sports. You can play alone or with a friend, using a (3) .................., where one person is on the left and the other on the right. When it was released, people were amazed that the system's (4) .................. could (5) .................. their movements. This, and the system's great (6) .................., which is fun for all ages, has made the Wii the market leader in its field.

**2** Work with another pair. Describe a computer game to the group. Use as many words from **1** as possible.

*Prisoner B12 is a first person, shoot 'em up game...*

## READING

**1 a** Work in groups. Read the introduction to the article. Write three things that you think Ren Yoshida will talk about.

**b** Read the rest of the article and check your ideas.

**2** Match topic sentences a–d to paragraphs 1–4.

a There's another stereotype that I'd like to challenge.
b Finally, I'd like to look at the issue of computers and childhood obesity.
c It's important to note that computer games are not just for fun.
d Are computer games bad for kids? Absolutely not!

**3** Are the sentences true or false according to the article? Correct the false sentences.

1 Computer games can prevent young people developing social skills.
2 You have to play most computer games by yourself.
3 Female characters in games are often weak and helpless.
4 Lara Croft has a positive influence on girls.
5 Computer games teach you that you need to make an effort to achieve things.
6 Literature teaches us about narrative and character, but computer games don't.
7 Many children are overweight because they spend too much time playing computer games.

# Game On!

*With the media again criticizing computer games for their bad influence on today's youth,* **Ren Yoshida** *looks at the other side of the argument.*

1 ………………… People who believe this obviously didn't grow up playing computer games. If you look at a first person, shoot 'em up game in a store, it looks like a solitary game. But according to research, about 60% of gamers play with friends. They take turns playing and giving advice, so it's a social activity, not one that isolates people. In any case, most computer games these days have at least some multiplayer functionality. And in case you hadn't realized it, part of the success of the Wii console is that it is fun for the whole family, old and young.

2 ………………… Computer games are not just a male activity. In fact, there is evidence that more girls than boys now play computer games online. This should be no surprise as games designers have always been ahead of the movie business in providing positive role models for girls. Female game characters are often portrayed as powerful and independent. Look at the classic platform game, *Tomb Raider*. It's famous not only for its impressive graphics but also for its fabulous main character. Lara Croft is a great role model for girls: she's tough and intelligent and leads an exciting international life.

3 ………………… They also teach a great deal. Most systems need to have simple gameplay to help people start quickly. But afterward, users need to gain the confidence and determination to go up a level. This teaches us that in order to accomplish more in life, we need to up our game! In addition, computer games often have a strong narrative, so they teach people about storytelling, character and other things that we also learn from literature.

4 ………………… Many children don't do a lot of exercise these days, but it's wrong to blame this on computer games. Have you ever seen young kids jumping around with the controllers on their Wii system? With the new motion sensors on the next generation of consoles, the machine can even read the players' movements without a control. With a split-screen game, two children can play and do exercise at the same time. So games aren't responsible for poor health. The biggest problem is that adults don't let their children go out and play in case something bad happens to them. You can't blame that on computer games.

**4** Find words or phrases in the article that mean...

1 done alone, without others *(adj) (para. 1).*
2 represented, shown *(past participle) (para. 2).*
3 strong, resilient *(adj) (para. 2).*
4 to complete, achieve *(v) (para. 3).*
5 to improve, increase *(v) (para. 3).*
6 medical condition of being overweight *(n) (para. 4).*

**5** Work in groups. Answer the questions.

- Do you agree with Ren Yoshida's opinions? Why/Why not?
- Imagine you had to argue against him. What points would you make?

## Speaking

**1** Work in groups. Think of other arguments for and against computer games. Complete the chart.

| For |
| --- |
| |

| Against |
| --- |
| |

**2** Present your arguments to the class. Which do you think are a) the strongest? b) the weakest? Why?

# 6.4 Functional Language: Generalizing

a

b

## Tune In

**1 a** Look at the images. What kind of music do you think you would hear in each place?

**b** Match images a and b to the definitions.

> **muzak** recorded background music that you hear in public places, e.g., in a store or restaurant
>
> **street performer** someone who entertains people for money in public places

**2 a** 6.5 Listen to two friends talking about music. Is their opinion generally positive or generally negative about a) street performers? b) background music?

**b** Listen again and answer the questions.

1 Why does George think people don't want to pay for music any more?
2 What three benefits of street performing does he mention?
3 Why does Camilla like street performers?
4 According to what Camilla has read, what are the benefits of playing background music in the workplace?
5 How does she say slow music affects shoppers?
6 What advantage can this have for store or restaurant owners?

## Focus on Language

**3 a** Complete the sentences with the phrases in the box.

| | | |
|---|---|---|
| the case | most cases | happens is |
| speaking | more often | a rule |

1 In .................., people just play music for themselves.
2 It's often .................. that musicians have two jobs.
3 .................. than not, they make *more* money from their other job.
4 What often .................., I end up performing on the streets.
5 Generally .................., people get more work done and feel happier.
6 As .................., the more time they spend in a store, the more they buy.

**b** 6.6 Listen and check.

**4** Use some of the phrases in 3 to make these statements into generalizations. Do you agree with the statements?

1 Everyone likes music of some kind.
2 Musicians learn to play an instrument at an early age.
3 Rock music today isn't as original as the old stuff.
4 People see street performers as poor and homeless.
5 Background music makes you feel more relaxed.

### Making generalizations

Listen to 6.6 again. Which words are stressed in the phrases for generalizing?

1 *In <u>most</u> cases...*

Listen again and repeat with the correct stress.

## Over to You

**5 a** Work in small groups. Choose one of the statements to discuss. Make general comments using a variety of phrases from 3.

- Music is too loud in bars and clubs.
- Television is much worse than it used to be.
- There's too much advertising in the world.

**b** Work with a student from a different group. Which statements did you discuss? What were the group's conclusions?

# Writing Task: A review

## Tune In

**1** **a** Work in pairs. Discuss the questions.

- Do you read reviews of movies, music or books?
- Where do you usually read them?
- Do you always trust the reviews you read? Why/Why not?

**b** Look at the image. What kind of DVD is it?

**2** **a** Read the review of *Life*. Is the writer's overall opinion positive or negative? Would you like to watch it?

**b** Underline two positive and two negative comments about the DVD.

## Prepare for Task

**3** Match functions a–g to paragraphs 1–4.

a positive points ..............
b description of content ..............
c negative points ..............
d conclusion/recommendation ..............
e catch reader's attention ..............
f favorite part ..............
g additional features ..............

**4** Answer the questions about the review.

1 Where would you read a review like this?
2 Is the style a) formal, b) semiformal or c) informal?

**5** **a** Match sentence halves 1–5 to a–e, without looking back at the review.

1 The best moment
2 Even if you aren't into this subject matter,
3 If there is a downside,
4 One other small complaint
5 But all in all,

a it's the music.
b this is an excellent package.
c is that the DVD box isn't very solid.
d is when the Komodo dragons hunt a buffalo.
e you'll find it completely absorbing.

**b** Check your answers in the review.

Posted by Renata Becagli • Nov 29, 2012

★★★★☆

**GREAT PRODUCT, GREAT PRICE!**

1 I don't usually like documentaries or wildlife programs because I find them really boring, but this one is an exception! *Life* is a series produced by the BBC showing the extraordinary lengths animals and plants go to in order to survive.

2 This is a stunning collection of some of the finest nature documentaries ever produced. The filming is spectacular—each scene is stunningly shot, edited and produced. In my opinion, the best moment is when the Komodo dragons hunt a buffalo and eat it! Even if you aren't into this subject matter, you'll find it completely absorbing. The commentary by David Attenborough is very informative, too. He makes complicated ideas easy to understand.

3 On the DVD itself, the menu is easy to use and there are plenty of extras, including a series of "making of" documentaries. If there is a downside, it's the music. There's just a little too much of it. One other small complaint is that the DVD box isn't very solid, and popping the discs out from the center is a little difficult!

4 For this reason, I gave the package four stars out of a possible five. But all in all, this is an excellent package, and I'd recommend it to anyone. You won't be disappointed!

» See more 5 star, 4 star reviews

## Task

**6** **a** Think of a movie, TV series, computer game or website that you would like to review. Prepare notes for each function in 3.

**b** Write your review. Organize it into paragraphs using the *Life* review as a guide. Use some of the phrases in 5a.

## Report Back

**7** Exchange reviews with a partner. Answer the questions.

1 Would you like to watch/read the subject of the review?
2 Does the review give enough information?
3 Do you think it's a fair review?

➔ Go to Review B, Unit 6, p. 70

## VOCABULARY

### Appearance

**1 a** Complete the sentences with appropriate verbs.

1 My daughter wants to ............ a piercing —in her eyebrow!
2 My 16-year-old brother's going to ............ his head because all his friends are doing it.
3 I just started playing football and need to ............ muscle. What's the best way to do this?
4 Carla only just met her boyfriend, but she wants to ............ a tattoo of his name on her arm!
5 My dad just retired, and now he wants to ............ his look to a more informal one.

**b** Work in pairs. Choose two sentences from 1a and act out a short conversation. How would you react to the news in each situation?

### Describing people

**2 a** Replace the words in bold with a synonym.

1 I'm very **chatty** when I'm with my friends.
2 I feel **shy and insecure** when I meet new people.
3 I usually feel **certain of success** before doing an exam. I always expect to pass.
4 I'm not as **funny and quick thinking** in English as I am in my own language.
5 I'm very **relaxed** about life. I don't get stressed about many things!

**b** Work in pairs. Are the sentences in 2a true for you?

**3** Think of four more adjectives to describe people. Are they positive or negative?

## GRAMMAR

### Present perfect or past simple?

**1 a** Write questions using the prompts. Add two more questions of your own.

1 ever / get / a piercing or tattoo?
2 when / last time / go to the beauty salon? what / have done?
3 anyone you know / change jobs / recently?
4 see / the latest Woody Allen movie yet?

**b** Work in groups of three. Ask and answer the questions. Find out as much information as possible.

### Present perfect simple or continuous?

**2 a** Choose the correct option to complete the blog post.

Over the last six months, I've (1)*taken / been taking* an intensive English course. We've (2)*had / been having* three different teachers so far. My speaking has (3)*improved / been improving* the most since I started. I still find it difficult to talk on the phone, though! This week I've (4)*moved / been moving*—I'm nearly finished now. There was a lot to organize and my phone has (5)*rung / been ringing* all the time. I've (6)*spoken / been speaking* to the real estate agent three times, but it was really hard to understand her.

**b** Work in pairs. Talk about something you have been learning recently. How long have you been doing it for? What has improved most?

### Uses of the *-ing* form

**3** Work in pairs. Write sentences that are true for you.

1 I'm really not looking forward to... because...
2 I need to practice... much more if I want to improve.
3 ... is my favorite weekend activity.
4 Next year, I'm going to concentrate on...

## FUNCTIONAL LANGUAGE

### Complaining

**1 a** Work in pairs. Complete the conversations.

1 A This video link is really ............ on my ............! It keeps stopping for no reason!
B Well, it is free, so you can't complain!

2 A I can't ............ the ............ my mother-in-law is always criticizing me!
B It's best to ignore it—try not to let her get to you.

3 A What ............ me the ............ is bad service in restaurants.
B Well, waiters aren't very well paid, so it's not surprising.

4 A The next-door neighbor's dog is ............ me ............! It barks all night long.
B There's not much you can do about noise if you live in an apartment.

**b** R6 Listen and check. Do you agree with B's responses?

**2** Work in groups. What annoys you most a) online? b) about services in your country? c) about where you live?

### LOOKING BACK

- What did you find most difficult in this unit? Why?
- Think of ten useful words to describe someone's appearance or personality.
- Have you been doing anything new this year that you've never done before? What is it? Tell a partner.

# VOCABULARY

## Food

**1** R7 Listen and match the description to the correct image a–d. List four ingredients used in the dish.

**2** **a** Work in pairs. Think of two adjectives to describe each dish in the other images in **1**.

*1 crunchy,...*

**b** Answer the questions with your ideas.

1 How were the dishes in the images cooked?
2 What spices or seasoning were used?
3 Which of the dishes would you most like to try? Why?

## Business

**3** **a** Work in groups of three. Can you name...

1 the most expensive brand of clothing in the world?
2 the largest multinational company?
3 the product that has greatest brand loyalty?
4 the most expensive type of franchise to start?
5 three factors a company uses to identify target markets (e.g., age)?

**b** Check your answers on page 158. Which group had the most correct answers?

# GRAMMAR

## Future forms

**1** **a** Complete the e-mail with an appropriate form of the verbs in parentheses. More than one future form may be possible.

File Edit View Tools Message Help

Hi Claudia,
Next week, I (1) .................... *(be)* in San Diego for a sales conference. I (2) .................... *(stay)* there for three days, so it would be great to get together. I think I (3) .................... *(have)* Thursday evening free as the sessions that day (4) .................... *(finish)* at 5:30. My flight (5) .................... *(leave)* at 1:30 p.m. on Friday. I (6) .................... *(call)* you when I arrive tomorrow night. Guess what! My sister's studying medicine at UCLA and she (7) .................... *(graduate)* next summer. Remember how bad she was at school! Hope to see you on Friday! Alex X

**b** Compare your answers with a partner's. Were they the same? If not, are both answers possible?

## Clauses

**2** **a** Complete the sentences so they are true for you.

1 As soon as I .................... , I .................... .
2 Before I .................... , I usually .................... .
3 Once I've .................... , I .................... .
4 I .................... this weekend unless .................... .
5 I don't think .................... will improve until .................... .

**b** Compare your answers with a partner's. Ask follow-up questions to find out more information.

## Future continuous/Future perfect

**3** Work in pairs. Ask and answer the questions. Give two answers for each one.

1 What will you be doing this/next summer?
2 What will you have done by then?

# FUNCTIONAL LANGUAGE

## Checking understanding

**1** **a** Work in pairs. Correct one mistake in each sentence.

1 Am I right for thinking that's a type of taco?
2 Does that have sense?
3 Can I just to check something?
4 One thing I don't understand is why do you say "hot dog"...
5 Do you see what I'm meaning?
6 Can you just tell that again?

**b** R8 Listen to the conversation and check your answers. What are the speakers talking about?

**2** **a** Work in pairs. Think of a typical dish from your country. Describe it to your partner and tell him/her how it is served.

Student A, check that your partner understands.
Student B, check any information you're not sure about.

**b** Switch roles and act out the conversation again.

## LOOKING BACK

- Which reading or listening text in this unit did you find most worrying? Why?
- Think of the last time you tried food from another country. Can you describe it to a partner?
- Think of three useful phrases for checking information. When do you think you might use them?

## VOCABULARY

### Entertainment

**1** Work in pairs. Which of these entertainers do you enjoy watching a) most? b) least? Why?

circus performer magician mime artist
puppeteer stand-up comedian
street performer

**2** Work in groups. Discuss the questions. Give reasons for your answers.

1 What's more important for the success of a movie/play—a strong cast or a good script?
2 Which actor do you think gave the best performance in a movie/play you saw recently?
3 What's your favorite movie soundtrack?
4 Which movie has the most impressive special effects?

**3** **a** Replace the words in bold with another adjective.

1 *The comedy gig last night* was **really funny**. I couldn't stop laughing!
2 I love watching *classical ballet*; I find it really **emotional**.
3 The most **exciting and absorbing** movie I've seen recently is *The Skin I Live in*.
4 I watched *a documentary about Bengal tigers last night*. It was truly **unforgettable**.

**b** Work in pairs. Change the information in italics so the sentences are true for you.

### Computer games

**4** **a** Choose the correct options.

One of the best video games ever made is **Legend of Zelda: Ocarina of Time**. It's a mixture of puzzle solving and sword-based combat. The enhanced (1)*graphics / stages* are incredibly realistic, especially in the version for the Nintendo 3DS (2)*console / controller*. Music plays an important role. To go up a (3)*level / platform*, the player must learn to play several songs on an ocarina (a type of flute). Another important aspect of (4)*gameplay / graphics* is exploration—players must obtain new items to explore certain areas. This is a (5)*shoot 'em up / first person* game, so players solve puzzles and look around the game world by controlling the main character, Link.

**b** Have you played/Would you like to play Legend of Zelda? Why/Why not?

## GRAMMAR

### The passive voice

**1** **a** Complete the review with the correct form, active or passive, of the verbs in parentheses.

It (1)............................ *(claim)* that Clint Eastwood is already a movie legend. *Gran Torino* (2008) (2)............................ *(direct)* by Eastwood, who also (3)............................ *(star)* in the movie. Eastwood (4)............................ *(play)* the role of a retired auto worker and Korean War veteran. He (5)............................ *(help)* the son of his Hmong neighbors, who (6)............................ *(try)* to steal his car: a Gran Torino. The movie (7)............................ *(set)* in Detroit and it (8)............................ *(give)* positive reviews. It (9)............................ *(consider)* to be one of Eastwood's best movies.

**b** R9 Listen and check. Then work in pairs. Tell your partner about a movie you have seen recently. Talk about...

- the director
- location
- main story
- actors/characters
- reviews

### *Have something done*

**2** Work in pairs. Discuss the questions.

1 What was the last thing you/your family had done to the place where you live?
2 When did you last get your hair cut? What did you have done?
3 Have you ever had something made for you? If so, what was it?

## FUNCTIONAL LANGUAGE

### Generalizing

**1** **a** Choose the correct option to complete the sentences.

1 As *a rule / happens*, I don't go to live concerts as they're too expensive.
2 More often *the case / than not*, big groups charge a fortune for the tickets.
3 What often *happens / speaking* is you end up kilometers away from the stage.
4 And in *the case / most cases*, the sound isn't great.
5 Generally *speaking / the case*, I'd rather listen to classical music than rock music.

**b** R10 Listen and check. Are the sentences in 1a true for you/ live music in your country?

**2** Work in groups of three. Use the phrases in 1a to generalize about another topic of your choice.

### LOOKING BACK

- Which task do you remember most clearly from this unit? Why?
- Think of four new phrases you have learned to talk about entertainment.
- Tell a partner about something you have had done for you recently. Why didn't you do it yourself?

## LISTENING

**1 a** Look at the ad for a language course. Complete the definition with your own words.

*A fluent speaker can...*

**b** Compare your sentences in small groups. Work together to write a definition for "fluency."

**2 a** R11 Listen to some learners' views on speaking English. Match questions 1–3 to a speaker/speakers.

R = Rikhil A = Agata F = Frank
N = Narumi C = Chenoa

Whose ideas...
1 are ambitious?
2 do you not agree with?
3 are similar to your own ideas?

**b** Compare your ideas with a partner's. Give reasons for your answers in 2a.

**3 a** Choose the correct option to complete the extracts.

1 I*'m going to* / *will* work hard to sound like a native speaker.
2 More often *than* / *that* not, people want to have a British accent.
3 I expect *being* / *to be* corrected by my teacher, too.
4 I hope I'll *have passed* / *be passing* the advanced speaking exam by this time next year.
5 I don't mind as long as people understand me—you know what I *mean* / *'m meaning*?
6 Recently I've *been making* / *made* an effort to be more outgoing in order to practice my conversation skills.

**b** Listen again and check.

## SPEAKING

**4** Work in pairs. Ask and answer the questions.

1 What would you like your speaking skills to be like in three years' time?
2 Which areas of speaking do you need to work on most?
- talking faster with fewer pauses
- communicating your ideas more clearly
- having clearer pronunciation
- speaking with fewer grammatical errors
- using more natural phrases/expressions

3 What ways of improving these areas can you think of?

## WRITING

**5 a** Write an action plan for improving/developing your speaking skills. Use these sentence stems if you like.

I need to be able to...
For this reason, I'd like to work on...
I'm going to do this by...
In three years' time, I'll be able to...

**b** Exchange plans with a partner. Are there any ideas that you would like to add to your action plan?

## QUICK CHECK

Complete the checklist below.

| Can you... | Yes, I can. | Yes, more or less. | I need to look again. |
|---|---|---|---|
| 1 describe changes in appearance? | ☐ | ☐ | ☐ |
| 2 talk about life experiences and changes? | ☐ | ☐ | ☐ |
| 3 complain about annoying situations? | ☐ | ☐ | ☐ |
| 4 describe food and ways to prepare it? | ☐ | ☐ | ☐ |
| 5 talk about future events, plans and intentions? | ☐ | ☐ | ☐ |
| 6 discuss different types of entertainment? | ☐ | ☐ | ☐ |
| 7 talk about hobbies and cultural heritage? | ☐ | ☐ | ☐ |
| 8 check understanding and clarify information? | ☐ | ☐ | ☐ |

Compare your answers with a partner's.

- What else do you know now after studying units 4–6?
- Do you need to look again at any of the sections?
- Do you need any extra help from your teacher?

# UNIT 1 GRAMMAR REFERENCE

## 1.1 AUXILIARY VERBS REVIEW

1 Use auxiliary verbs *be* and *have* with a main verb to form tenses.
*be* = continuous tenses:
*The Internet is working now.*
*have* = perfect tenses:
*I haven't seen Jo today.*

2 In questions and negatives, use the auxiliary verb *do* to form the present simple and *did* to form the past simple:
*We don't know the answer.*
*Did you go to the party?*

3 In affirmative sentences in the present simple and past simple, we can use *do*/*did* to emphasize the main verb. The auxiliary is always stressed in spoken language:
*I did tell you about the field trip on Friday!*

We also use auxiliary verbs...

4 in short answers to questions:
*Do you have a Facebook account? Yes, I do./No, I don't.*

5 with pronouns (*he*, *she*, etc.) to make question tags:
*He's spent a lot of time online this week, hasn't he?*

### Subject questions

Where the question word (*what*, *who*, etc.) is the subject of a question, we do not use an auxiliary verb in the present simple or past simple:

*Who told you about the new website?* (NOT *Who ~~did tell~~ you...*)

## 1.2 PAST PARTICIPLES

The past participle is the third form of the verb: *go*, *went*, *gone*. We form regular past participles by adding *-ed* to the infinitive. Many verbs have irregular past participles (see page 168 for a list of common ones).

We use the past participle...

| | |
|---|---|
| 1 with *have* to form the present perfect and past perfect | *Anna's just sent me an e-mail. I hadn't heard from her for weeks.* |
| 2 with *be* to form the passive voice | *The mail is delivered at 10 a.m. every day.* |
| 3 to form adjectives | *The hotel has a heated pool.* |
| 4 with *have* + object to describe something that is done for or to you | *I need to have my eyes checked.* |
| 5 with *have* + object to describe something bad that happens to you | *He didn't pay his bills, so he had his electricity cut off.* |

## 1.3 REFLEXIVE PRONOUNS

We use reflexive pronouns...

1 when the subject and object of a verb are the same person or thing:
*She made herself a cup of tea.*
Some verbs that commonly go with reflexive pronouns are:
*ask blame enjoy express give*
*hurt introduce take care of teach*

2 to mean "without help from other people":
*My team members were sick, so I had to finish the project myself.*

### 1.1

**a** Correct one mistake in each sentence or mini-dialogue.

1 How many brothers or sisters you have?
2 A: Did you speak to Kim yesterday?
B: Yes, I have.
3 Barbara does speaks German! She studied it in college.
4 How many times you have been to the USA?
5 Who did invented Twitter?
6 A: Who leave this note on my desk?
B: Sam did.

**b** Complete the dialogues with the correct question tags.

1
A You're not on Twitter, ........ ........ ?
B I'm not, but you use Facebook, ........ ........ ?

2
A You've met my roommate Agata before, ........ ........ ?
B I think so. She's the one with the piercings, ........ ........ ?

3
A Could you help me with this report, Sarah?
B Of course! The boss is demanding a lot from you right now, ........ ........ ?

### 1.2

**a** Complete the dialogue with the past participle form of the verbs in the box.

abuse fix hear improve realize tell

A I've just been ........ that the company is only letting us use the Internet for one hour a day! Have you ........ anything about it?
B So that's why I can't get onto MySpace. I hadn't ........ there was the new rule. I was about to call IT to have my computer ........ .
A Well, I think it's ridiculous! I feel as if I've had my human rights ........ or something.
B That's kind of an exaggeration! I can see their reasons. They might actually get a new, ........ workforce!

**b** Match the use of each past participle in **a** to rules 1–5 in Grammar Reference 1.2.

### 1.3

**a** Write the missing reflexive pronoun in the correct position in each sentence.

1 My brothers never ask if they can borrow my things. They just help.
2 When I have a problem, I'd rather deal with it than talk it over with friends or family.
3 My friend Larry is so shy! He finds it hard to introduce to people he doesn't know.
4 My mother always blames when things go wrong!
5 It's nice to go on vacation with friends, but sometimes my wife and I prefer to just go by.

**b** Are any of the sentences in **a** true for you or anyone you know?

## 2.1 THE PRESENT

### Present simple

Use the present simple...

| | |
|---|---|
| 1 to talk about habits and routines | *She works late every day.* |
| 2 to describe things that are generally true | *In the U.S., most people have a big meal in the evening.* |
| 3 to talk about scheduled events | *The post office closes at 3 p.m.* |

### Present continuous

Use the present continuous...

| | |
|---|---|
| 1 to talk about things that are happening at the time of speaking | *Why are they laughing?* |
| 2 to talk about temporary situations happening around now | *She's studying for her final exams.* |
| 3 to talk about changing or developing situations | *My Spanish is really improving.* |
| 4 for repeated habits or actions that cause annoyance, often with adverbs such as *always, constantly* | *He's constantly telling me to exercise more.* |

**NOTE:** We do not usually use the present continuous with state verbs, e.g., *know, like, believe.*

### Present perfect

In general, the present perfect is used to talk about events or states that take place in the past but have a connection to, or result in, the present:

*They've torn down the old theater to build a new freeway.*

We often use time expressions to show the past–present link:

*all my life, recently, today, lately, over the last few months/years, up to now, this week/month/year, since last week, for a year*

## 2.2 USED TO DO/USED TO DOING

### Used to + infinitive

Use *used to* + infinitive to talk about habits, states or repeated actions in the past, which are often no longer true in the present:

*We used to go on vacation with my uncle.* (now we don't)

Notice how we form the negative and question form with *used to*:

*Did you **use** to play basketball when you were a kid?*

*No, I didn't **use** to like sports that much.*

In tag questions with *used to*, use the auxiliary *did* in the question tag:

*You used to play the piano, didn't you?*

### Be/Get used to + -ing

1 Use *be used to* to talk about things that are familiar and no longer strange or difficult for us.

2 Use *get used to* to talk about things that become more familiar and less strange/difficult over time.

*Be/Get used to* can be followed by...

a) a noun/noun phrase or pronoun:

*We're not used to the new telephone system.*

b) a verb in the *-ing* form:

*I got used to getting up early for my yoga class.*



### 2.1

**a** Complete the sentences with the correct present tense forms of the verb in parentheses.

1 **Every afternoon** Neil .................... out for a long walk with his grandmother. *(go)*

2 I .................... to school **this month** to get in shape. *(walk)*

3 I played squash **yesterday,** and I think I .................... a muscle in my arm! It's agony! *(pull)*

4 **What time** .................... the dance class .................... ? *(start)*

5 I .................... of giving up my gym membership. *(think)*

6 I .................... two kilograms **since last month**! *(lose)*

**b** Write sentences that are true for you, using the phrases in bold in **a**.

**c** Find and correct six mistakes in the e-mail.

New | Reply | Reply all | Forward | Delete | Junk | Sweep • Mark as • Move to •

Hi Ben, thanks for your e-mail and the photos. I'm really liking the one of you dancing at the party! I'm pretty busy at the moment because I prepare for a big presentation next week. I'm normally having meetings every morning, but this week I having training sessions in the afternoons as well. I don't go for a run since last Sunday! You know how much I love run! At home it's hard to get any work done because my neighbor always listened to loud music. It's so annoying! How are things with you?
Write soon, Mandy

### 2.2

Choose the correct option a–c to complete the sentences.

1 I .................... really sick when I saw operations on TV, but now I'm a surgeon!
a) got used to feeling b) am used to feeling
c) used to feel

2 It's hard to .................... nights, but it becomes normal after a while.
a) used to work b) get used to working
c) be used to working

3 I .................... at all. I wasn't in good shape.
a) didn't use to exercise b) wasn't used to exercise
c) used to exercise

4 The job was really stressful at first, but now I .................... with difficult patients.
a) used to deal b) got used to dealing
c) 'm used to dealing

5 I'm slowly .................... English every day at work.
a) used to speak b) getting used to speaking
c) used to speaking

# UNIT 3 GRAMMAR REFERENCE

## 3.1 Narrative tenses

### Past simple & past continuous

1 Use the **past simple** to talk about completed actions that happened at a specific time in the past. These tell the main events of a story in the order they happened:
*He packed his bags, ordered a taxi and left the house for good.*

2 Use the **past continuous** to talk about...
a) background information that is not part of the main story:
*The sun was shining and the birds were singing.*
b) an action in progress around a particular time in the past, often when this is interrupted by another (shorter) action:
*I was making an important call when the fire alarm went off.*
c) two simultaneous actions or events, with connecting words such as *while, meanwhile*:
*While I was finishing my work, Gail was cooking dinner.*

### Past perfect simple & past perfect continuous

1 Use the **past perfect simple** to talk about...
a) an action that was completed before another action in the past:
*When I opened my bag I realized that I'd (had) left my ticket at home.*
b) a state or situation in progress up to a point of time in the past:
*They'd been friends for years until she moved away from the area.*
NOTE: The emphasis is on completion, not duration.

2 Use the **past perfect continuous** to talk about...
a) an ongoing action that started before another action in the past (and often continued up to it):
*The miners had been digging all night when they heard the explosion.*
b) repeated actions that happened before another action in the past:
*I'd been calling all morning before I finally got a hold of her.*
NOTE: The emphasis is on duration.

## 3.2 Adverbs

We can use adverbs...

1 to say how we do something (adverbs of manner). These usually go at the end of a clause/sentence:
*I pick up new languages quickly.*

2 to say how often we do something (adverbs of frequency). These usually go before a main verb or after *to be* or another auxiliary verb:
*I never go on extreme rides at amusement parks.*
*I don't usually do outdoor activities on the weekend.*

3 to modify an adjective. These go before the adjective they modify:
*Cantonese is an incredibly difficult language to learn.*

4 to describe a whole sentence (sentence adverbs). These often show the speaker's/writer's attitude to what is being said. They commonly go at the beginning of a sentence:
*Tragically, many lives were lost in the accident.*
*Surprisingly, he's decided not to leave after all.*



**3.1**

**a** Choose the correct verb form to complete the sentences.

1 The climber *crawled / was crawling* all the way back to camp after he *was breaking / had broken* his leg.
2 I'd never *been doing / done* any sailing before, and I must admit I *wasn't liking / didn't like* it at all!
3 We'd *been walking / walked* for hours before we *were finding / found* someone to help us.
4 When I *fell / had been falling* out of the boat, I *was screaming / screamed* for help, and luckily the lifeguard *had seen / saw* me.

**b** Complete the text with the verbs in parentheses in the correct narrative tense.

## Rescued by Fire Ants

In 1999, Joan Murray (1) .................. *(skydive)* when her main parachute (2) .................. *(fail)* to open during a jump from 4,420 meters. Her backup chute (3) .................. *(open)* when she was 200 meters above the ground, but then it deflated. Joan (4) .................. *(crash)* to the ground and the impact (5) .................. *(smash)* the side of her body. Amazingly, she was still alive when rescuers found her! She (6) .................. *(land)* on a mound of fire ants, and doctors believe the stings from the ants (7) .................. *(shock)* her heart so that it (8) .................. still .................. *(beat)* and saved her life. She (9) .................. *(be)* in a coma for two weeks, but she (10) .................. *(heal)* well enough to go home after six weeks.

**3.2**

**a** Complete the sentences with an adverb in the box in the correct position.

| badly | easily | extremely | personally | rarely |
|---|---|---|---|---|

1 I watch horror movies. Some are really terrifying.
2 I don't get scared, so I love any kind of extreme sport.
3 It's dangerous to drive over 120 km/h on the highway.
4 I think jumping off a bridge with a piece of elastic tied around your leg is really stupid.
5 I sing, so I'd love to take lessons to improve.

**b** Change the sentences in **a** so they are true for you or reflect your opinion.

## 4.1 Present perfect or past simple?

1 Use the **present perfect** for events that connect the past to the present. We can use it...

a) for experiences in our lives up to now, when we don't specify a point in time:

*I've been to India, but I've never been to Thailand.*

b) a state or action that started in the past and continues up to now:

*I've had this website for two years.*

c) with *already* in affirmative sentences and questions to mean "before now," especially to express surprise:

*Have you finished your assignment already?*

d) with *yet* in negative sentences and questions to talk about events that have not happened up to now but that we expect to happen in the future:

*Have you shown Lucy the website yet? No, I haven't seen her yet.* (= I expect to see her in the future.)

2 Use the **past simple...**

a) to talk about completed past events that happened at a specific time in the past:

*I watched a great movie on TV last night.*

b) a repeated, habitual action in the past:

*I watched a lot of cartoons when I was a child.*

## 4.2 Present perfect simple or continuous?

The present perfect simple emphasizes completion:

*I've written an article for the website.* (= it's finished)

The present perfect continuous emphasizes duration:

*I've been writing a book about Latin America.* (= I'm still writing it)

We use the present perfect simple to talk about how many things we have done or how many times we have done something:

*I've sent 25 e-mails today. I've e-mailed John twice.*

We use the present perfect continuous to talk about how long we have been doing something:

*I've been sending e-mails all morning.*

We also use the present perfect continuous for a recently finished action with a present result:

*He's exhausted because he's been working all night.*

## 4.3 Uses of the *-ing* form

The *-ing* form of a verb (gerund) sometimes acts like a noun. Use it

| | |
|---|---|
| 1 as the subject of a sentence | *Swimming is a great form of exercise.* |
| 2 after a preposition | *I'm interested in hearing about your trip!* |
| 3 after certain verbs, e.g., *like, love, hate, enjoy, avoid, consider, imagine, practice* | *I love traveling, but I avoid going anywhere on official holidays.* |
| 4 after an article or *my, your, his,* etc. | *Her singing is really good.* |
| 5 after "no" on warning notices | *No running in the hallways!* |

### 4.1

Complete the profile with the correct form of the verbs: past simple or present perfect.

**Profile**

Hi! I'm Paul Channing and I (1) .......... *(have)* this website since I was 16. I (2) .......... *(start)* writing it back in 2008 when I (3) .......... *(graduate)* school and (4) .......... *(decide)* to work my way around the world. I (5) .......... *(have)* lots of different jobs over the last few years. My first one, in 2009, (6) .......... *(be)* as a dishwasher in Australia —I (7) .......... *(wash)* dishes in a really busy kitchen! Since then, I (8) .......... *(be)* a tour guide in Shanghai, a waiter in London and even a driver in South Africa! In fact, last January I (9) .......... *(meet)* my girlfriend in Cape Town. She loves traveling, too, and she (10) .......... *(already/buy)* tickets for our next trip—a walking tour of Morocco. We (11) .......... *(not decide)* what jobs we want to do there yet but I'm sure there are plenty of options.

### 4.2

**a** Choose the best option to complete the sentences.

1 They've *surfed / been surfing* at the beach for hours.
2 My aunt has *written / been writing* a book about Ancient Greece. She's on the last chapter.
3 You're soaking wet! What have you *done / been doing*?
4 I've *visited / been visiting* my grandfather a lot recently as he's not very well.
5 Sammi's *seen / been seeing* her therapist three times this week!
6 Have you *told / been telling* your boss you're leaving?

**b** Write true sentences to answer the questions.

1 What have you been doing a lot recently?
2 How many movies have you seen this month?
3 Have you taken up a new hobby or interest recently? How long have you been doing it for?

### 4.3

**a** Find and correct one mistake in each sentence. One sentence is already correct.

1 **I'm not used to** stay up late at night.
2 **I don't know anything about** fix cars.
3 My dad's cooking **is great—much better than** my mom's!
4 **I'm really look forward to** seeing my friends tonight.
5 **I'm not very good at** remember names.
6 No eat in the theater.

**b** Write five sentences that are true for you, using the correct form of the phrases in bold in **a**.

# UNIT 5 GRAMMAR REFERENCE

## 5.1 Future forms

A common mistake in English is to overuse *will* to talk about the future. We most often use *will* for...

1 general predictions and opinions about the future:
*Don't bother buying a lottery ticket. You won't win.*

2 offers, promises or spontaneous plans/decisions:
*I'll buy dinner next time!*

More than one future form is often possible in similar situations.

1 We can make a prediction using *will* or *going to*:
*He'll find/He's going to find retirement difficult!*
**Note:** We often use *going to* for predictions based on present evidence:
*Look at that rock! It's going to fall.*

2 We can describe a future plan or arrangement using *going to* or the present continuous: *We're interviewing/We're going to interview candidates for the new job next week.*
**Note:** We often use the present continuous for fixed future arrangements and *going to* for plans or intentions where no actual arrangement has been made. We use the present simple for scheduled future events.

## 5.2 Clauses

A sentence can contain a main clause and a second (or subordinate) clause that gives more information. We can add a subordinate clause to a main clause with words like: *as soon as, before/after, once, unless, until*:

*I'll go for coffee after/once/as soon as I finish this e-mail.*

If the verb in the main clause is with *will* or *going to*, the verb in the subordinate clause is in the present simple or present perfect:

*I'll call you as soon as I arrive.*

*We'll take the kids to the park once they've done their homework.*

## 5.3 Future continuous/perfect

### Future continuous

Use the future continuous...

1 to describe an action in progress at a point in the future:
*This time next week, we'll be flying to Rio.*

2 to speculate about what someone is doing at the moment of speaking:
*My parents will be watching the news now.*

We form the future continuous with *will* + *be* + the *-ing* form of the verb:

| | |
|---|---|
| + | *I'll be lying on a beach this time next week.* |
| – | *I won't be working.* |
| Y/N | *Will you be checking your e-mails? Yes, I will. / No, I won't.* |

### Future perfect

Use the future perfect to describe an action that will be completed before a point of time in the future:

*By the end of 2020, my grandparents will have been married for fifty years!*

We form the future perfect with *will* + *have* + past participle:

| | |
|---|---|
| + | *I'll have written the report by Thursday.* |
| – | *I won't have confirmed the meeting.* |
| Y/N | *Will you have confirmed it by Friday? Yes, I will. / No, I won't.* |

**5.1**

**a** Complete the answers to the question with an appropriate future form of the verbs in parentheses. More than one answer may be possible.

**What are you doing tonight?**

1 I haven't thought about it. I .................... my friends now to find out their plans. *(text)*
2 Going home. My train .................... at 7 o'clock. *(leave)*
3 I think I .................... my friends in the café, but I'm not sure yet. *(meet)*
4 I'm staying home. Look at those clouds—it .................... . *(rain)*
5 I .................... my driving test. Wish me luck! *(take)*
6 I don't have any plans yet. I .................... Jan if he wants to go out. *(ask)*

**b** Write three sentences about your plans for tonight. Use a variety of future forms.

**5.2**

Link the sentences using the word in parentheses. Make any other necessary changes.

1 I get home at about four. I'll call you earlier.
(BEFORE) *I'll call you before I get home.*
2 I'm not going home right now. I need to speak to my teacher first.
(UNTIL) ....................
3 I'll buy some coconut milk later. Then we'll make a nice Thai curry.
(ONCE) ....................
4 I'm getting my test results tomorrow. I'll call you when I know what they are.
(AS SOON AS) ....................
5 You'll need to buy a ticket online. You can't get on the bus without one.
(UNLESS) ....................

**5.3**

Complete the dialogue with the correct form of the verbs in parentheses: future continuous or future perfect.

**A** Just think, this time next week we .................... *(finish)* our exams and we .................... *(fly)* home!
**B** I know, I can't wait! I'm not looking forward to the long flight, though. We .................... *(sit)* down for hours. It's so boring and uncomfortable.
**A** Oh, don't worry, you .................... *(feel)* so tired that you'll sleep most of the way. It's our going away party the day before, so we probably .................... *(sleep)* much!
**B** That's true. I'm looking forward to having some real Brazilian food again! On Saturday night, I .................... *(sit)* in that restaurant near the harbor. I won't be able to move as I .................... *(eat)* so much feijoada!
**A** Oh stop it! You're making me hungry!

## 6.1 THE PASSIVE VOICE

To form the passive, use an appropriate form of *be* + past participle:

*More movies are made in India than in Hollywood.*

*Many westerns have been filmed in Spain.*

*More movies will be made in 3D in the future.*

Use *by* to emphasize the person or thing responsible for the action:

*The movie was directed by Pedro Almodóvar.*

*The lead role is played by Antonio Banderas.*

Do not use *by*:

| | |
|---|---|
| 1 when it's obvious who/ what is responsible for the action | *It was filmed in Italy.* (by the movie crew) |
| 2 when we don't know who/what is responsible for the action | *Expensive equipment has been stolen.* (we don't know who by) |
| 3 to describe a process | *The cast is hired, locations are chosen and sets are built.* |

### With reporting verbs

Use *it* + the passive form of a reporting verb (*say*, *believe*, *think*, etc.) to express other people's opinions, without naming the exact source:

*It is widely recognized that Charlie Chaplin was a comic genius.*

*It is often claimed that* Citizen Kane *is the best movie ever made.*

## 6.2 *HAVE SOMETHING DONE*

### Use

Use *have* + object + past participle to describe...

1 an action that we arrange for another person to do for us:

*We've had our photo taken for the website.*

*When are you going to have your hair cut?*

2 a bad experience that happens to us:

*They've had their new car stolen.*

*I had my electricity cut off.*

**NOTE:** We can use *get* instead of *have*. It is common in informal spoken English and in imperatives:

*Get your car washed! It's filthy.*

### Form

| | |
|---|---|
| present simple | *I have my paper delivered every morning.* |
| present continuous | *We're having our bathroom painted.* |
| past simple | *I had the house cleaned last week.* |
| present perfect | *You've had your hair cut!* |
| present perfect continuous | *She's been having a new kitchen designed.* |
| future with *will* | *I'll have my car repaired this weekend.* |

### 6.1

**a** Rewrite the sentences using the passive voice. Use *by* where necessary.

1 One of my students gave me this necklace.
*I was given this necklace by one of my students.*

2 Someone has hacked into my e-mail account!
..................

3 Someone was selling these tickets outside the concert hall.
..................

4 Many people believe he is the greatest actor of our generation.
..................

5 My grandmother told that joke—can you believe it?
..................

6 Some people say that stand-up comedy is one of the most terrifying things you can do.
..................

**b** Complete the movie review by writing the underlined verbs in the correct form (active or passive, present simple or past simple).

**The Departed** is a 2006 American crime thriller. It is a remake of the 2002 Hong Kong movie *Infernal Affairs*. While remakes *are* always (1) *compared* compare to the original, this particular movie (2) talk about more than most because it (3) direct by the great Martin Scorsese and (4) star Hollywood greats such as Leonardo DiCaprio, Matt Damon and Jack Nicholson. The movie (5) set in Boston, Massachusetts and follows the story of a police officer and a young criminal who both (6) lead double lives. It (7) nominate for 12 Oscars, and (8) it win five, including Best Picture and Best Director. However, it (9) claim that Scorsese (10) give the award only because he had been nominated so many times before and never won!

### 6.2

Complete the sentences with the correct form of *have* and a verb in the box.

decorate ~~fix~~ make take test steal

1 Instead of buying a new bike, why don't you just *have* your old one *fixed*?
2 I absolutely hate .................. my photo .................. .
3 We're .................. the whole house .................. at the moment.
4 She's going to .................. her dress .................. by the same designer who made mine!
5 I .................. my eyes .................. yesterday. Apparently, I have perfect vision!
6 I couldn't call you because I've .................. my phone .................. .

# WRITING BANK

## 1 A QUESTION-AND-ANSWER POST

**1 a** Work in pairs. Read the question post. What suggestions would you give?

**YOUR QUESTIONS Topic:** Angry people

Open

**Sort by:** ▶ Newest ▶ Most Popular ▶ Fewest Answers

**Alex808** **What's the best way to deal with someone who is angry? I've just started working in customer service, so any advice would be appreciated!**

**b** Read the answer post below and answer the questions.

1 Are any of your suggestions from 1a mentioned? 2 Do you agree with the advice? Why/Why not?

It can be difficult dealing with someone who's really angry. I know I sometimes end up getting angry myself and then things can get out of hand. I've found it helpful to remember to stay calm and in control. What I do first is acknowledge the person's feelings, without agreeing or disagreeing with them. I say something like, "I can see you're really angry about this." Then I offer an apology, as this helps defuse the situation. Finally, when things have calmed down, I ask an open-ended question like, "What can I do to help?" This can help an angry person to be more rational. (In my experience, this only works if you have acknowledged their emotions first, though.) So my advice would be to remember the three "As" the next time you have to deal with an angry person: Acknowledge, Apologize, Ask a question. Hope you find this works for you! Good luck!

**2** Look at phrases a–f from the post. Which are used to...

1 describe what the writer does in this situation?
2 describe what the writer has done in this situation in the past?
3 give an example?
4 suggest what the other person should do?

a I know I sometimes... ......1......
b In my experience,... ............
c I say something like... ............
d I've found it helpful to... ............
e So my advice would be to... ............
f What I do first is... ............

**3** Work in pairs. You are going to write an online question-and-answer post. Write one question for each of these topics.

1 How to deal with over-protective parents
2 The best way to meet people in a new place
3 The effectiveness of social networks in making friends

**4 a** Exchange questions with another pair. Choose one question and write an answer post. Use the phrases in 2 if you like.

**b** Exchange answers with the same pair. Answer the questions.

1 Were the answers clear and relevant?
2 What would you change/add?

### TIP

Use an informal style in question-and-answer posts. If you write a question, it is polite (although not essential) to say that you will appreciate any advice others give you. If you write an answer, make sure it is polite, clear and easy to follow and based on your personal experience.

## 2 A TRAVEL BLOG

**1** **a** Work in pairs. You are going to read a travel blog. Before reading, discuss the questions.

1. Where is the Trans-Siberian Railway?
2. Where does it start and finish?
3. How long does it take to travel from one end to the other?

**b** Read the blog and check your answers.

**2** Find and underline this information in the blog.

| | |
|---|---|
| **Introduction:** | where and when the trip started; feelings about the trip |
| **Descriptions:** | traveling companions; places visited |
| **Actions:** | what the writer did during the trip |
| **Opinions:** | what he liked and didn't like |
| **Conclusion:** | how the trip ended; why he recommends this trip |

**3** Work in pairs. Read typical blog features 1–6. Do they apply to this blog?

1. Blog entries often talk about one topic.
2. They are usually fairly short.
3. They use a relaxed, informal style.
4. They express the feelings and opinions of the writer.
5. Most have space for comments and responses from readers.
6. They are arranged in chronological order, from the most recent entry at the top to older entries toward the bottom.

**4** Write a blog entry about a day sightseeing or a trip you made. Use the outline in 2 as a guide and incorporate some of the features in 3.

**5** Work in pairs. Exchange blog entries and answer the questions.

1. Is the writing style engaging? Why/Why not?
2. Is there any additional information you would like to have?

### TIP

When you write a blog post, make your opinions clear. People want to hear your voice and know what you think. Use a natural, conversational style. Think of someone you know well and imagine you are writing for him/her.

Profile | Blog | Photos | Videos | Messages

### My Trans-Siberia Journal

3 July, posted at 10:48 p.m.

I boarded the train in Moscow tonight and we set off at 21:30! Really excited to be on my way and taking this trip at last but also a little nervous. I'm in second class and am sharing the car with three other people.

4 July, posted at 3:24 p.m.

I made friends with my traveling companions last night. They're Ivan, Dasha and Katya, all Russians who don't speak much English. I broke the ice by showing them photos of family and friends. I also put a notepad and a Russian–English dictionary on the table. Thanks to the photos, we made friends quickly and used the dictionary and notepad to talk.

7 July, posted at 11:37 p.m.

I left the train at Irkutsk and took a bus to Listvyanka, a village on the shore of Lake Baikal. There are some beautiful old wooden houses and a few stores and restaurants. Early in the morning the harbor is full of local people smoking fresh fish to sell to villagers. Then I traveled back to Irkutsk and caught the train for the final leg of my trip.

10 July, posted at 10:09 p.m.

We arrived in Vladivostok late last night after six full days on the train! The only downside was the dining car. The food wasn't great and it was really expensive. Fortunately, in every station there were local people selling reasonably priced, homemade food, which was always delicious.

We've traveled through eight time zones and passed through some incredible places! I was so sad the trip was over. I would thoroughly recommend it! There's no better way to travel 9,000 kilometers, see amazing scenery and meet fellow travelers or locals.

**5 comments and 1 reaction**

## 3 A WIKI

**1** Work in pairs. Read the definition and answer the questions.

> **wiki** *(n)* a website that allows people to write or edit articles

1 Do you know of any other wikis, apart from Wikipedia?
2 Have you ever written or edited an article for a website like Wikipedia?

**2 a** Work in pairs. You are going to read a wiki article about Indian cuisine. What ingredients do you think it will mention?

**b** Read the wiki article and check your ideas in 2a. Are the ingredients used in a) main courses, b) desserts or c) drinks?

**3** Work in pairs. Identify four differences between northern and southern Indian cuisine.

**4** Read the wiki guidelines. Does the article follow them?

- Use a neutral, formal style: avoid *I, me*, etc.
- Do not use phrases like *of course*.
- Do not use adverbs that indicate emotions, like *incredibly*, *unbelievably*.
- Avoid overuse of exclamation marks.
- Use the passive to report information from other people: *It is said that...*

**5 a** Cover the wiki article. Rewrite the paragraph following the guidelines in 4a.

> If you go to India, you'll find lots of different regions, each with a specific cuisine. Amazingly, there is no single dish that people call "curry" in India! People suspect that *curry* is an English form of a word meaning *sauce*, and there are many varieties. Obviously, almost all of them are spicy.

**b** Compare your answer to the first paragraph in the wiki article.

**6 a** Choose types of cuisine from two regions in your country. Write a wiki article about them, using the plan.

**Introduction:** a general description of cuisine in your country
**Main sections:** popular main dishes—their ingredients and how they are prepared
a common dessert and drink

**b** Work in pairs. Exchange articles and answer the questions.

1 Is the article interesting? Why/Why not?
2 Is there enough/too much information? What would you change/add?

Article | Discussion

### Indian Cuisine

Every Indian region has a specific cuisine. Contrary to popular belief, there is no single dish known as "curry" in India. *Curry* is thought to be an English derivation of a word meaning "sauce," and there are many varieties. They tend to be spicy, using seasonings such as cardamom, ginger and turmeric.

**Northern cuisine**

The most popular dishes in northern India contain chicken and lamb. They are prepared with sauces made from chili, ginger or onions and then roasted in ovens called *tandoors*.

Nuts are a key ingredient in main courses and also in puddings. These are made with milk and sugar, sometimes mixed with yogurt or cream. Yogurt is also the main ingredient of the region's most popular drink, the *lassi*. In this region, breads such as *chapati* and *naan* usually accompany main courses.

**Southern cuisine**

Throughout the south, vegetarian dishes are common, and almost all meals are served with rice. Fish and seafood are also eaten in coastal areas, usually in a curry made from coconut and sesame. Coconut is one of the most popular refreshments, and its milk is typically drunk directly from the coconut. Although vegetarianism is common, meat dishes are also served, especially as part of *korma*, a creamy curry that may be made with lamb, chicken or fish. There are also many desserts. A famous one is *khubani ka meetha*, which combines apricots with ice cream.

**TIP**

Begin your wiki article with a simple introduction for people who just want a general understanding of the topic. Add more detailed information later, for those who require more in-depth knowledge.

# Communication Bank

## 2.3 Speaking, page 21, Exercise 2

**Student A**

**You are going to do a simple psychology experiment with your partner. Follow the instructions.**

**1** Show list 1 to your partner (cover list 2). Give him/her 30 seconds to read it.

**List 1:** ambulance, aspirin, backache, bed, hospital, sick, medicine, nurse, pharmacist, surgeon

**2** Cover list 1 and show your partner list 2. Can he/she identify which words were also in list 1?

**List 2:** acquaintance, ambulance, boss, computer, roommate, landscape, midwife, network, nurse, yellow

**3** Answer the questions together.

1 What was the result of the experiment?
2 What do you think the experiment is testing? Check your ideas on page 156.
3 Do you think the result would be the same if you did the experiment in your own language?

## Review B, Vocabulary, page 69, Exercise 3a

1 Hermes
2 HSBC
3 cigarettes
4 hotel or motel franchise
5 *(suggested answers)* income, family size, education, occupation, gender, nationality

## 2.3 Speaking, page 21, Exercise 2

**Experiment**

In this experiment, we learn about false memory. This is when we think we remember things from the past that weren't there or didn't happen. In this experiment, people often think they remember the word "midwife" from the first list because all the other words in list 1 are connected to medicine.

## 2.3 Speaking, page 21, Exercise 2

**Student B**

**Follow the instructions.**

1 Read the list of words your partner shows you in 30 seconds.
2 Read the second list. Which words in list 2 were also in list 1?
3 Answer the questions in Exercise 3 on page 158 with your partner.

### 1.3, p. 6, Ex 1b

**S** = Suzanne, **J** = Jacques,
**D** = Dave, **G** = Gina

1

**S:** OK, my first interview is with Jacques, my ex-roommate. Jacques, this is an interesting photo. It's your profile photo, isn't it? But why didn't you use one of yourself... you know, something more personal?

**J:** Well, I did think about it, but I felt a little shy, especially because I've changed a lot since college. I mean, the Eiffel Tower is more impersonal, but it's special to me. I used to work there, and I have great memories of it.

**S:** I remember! You sold tickets one summer, didn't you?

**J:** Yeah, exactly. I worked with fantastic people. We got along really well, and we're all still friends. So, I guess I posted this photo to remind me of a happy time in my life.

2

**S:** OK, Dave. Thanks for being on my podcast.

**D:** No problem, Suzanne.

**S:** I haven't seen this photo before...

**D:** You have seen it—you're in it! That's you in the middle! Don't you remember?

**S:** Oh yeah, I do! We were on the umm... the geography field trip just after our exams. Who's the guy on the left though? The one in the blue T-shirt... I don't remember him.

**D:** I think he was a friend of Nina's.

**S:** And, um... didn't something happen to him that day?

**D:** Yes, something did happen! He climbed a tree on a dare and fell out on the way down.

**S:** Oh yes! He didn't hurt himself, though, did he?

**D:** No, he didn't break anything... but he ended up having to go to the hospital for an X-ray.

**S:** I remember now... Poor thing, that was crazy!

3

**S:** This is typical of you and your friends, Gina!

**G:** Hey, no it's not! I don't always post pictures like this.

**S:** Yes, you do. I expected some nice artistic photos... and I get you and your friends on a night out.

**G:** OK, OK, I guess it's not artistic... but it's funny, isn't it?

**S:** Well, everyone does look like they're having fun. So... who took the photo?

**G:** My sister-in-law did.

**S:** And do you worry that people will see you out partying? What about, you know, your coworkers or your boss?

**G:** No, I don't. They can't see them! I'm very careful about the privacy settings on my account, so you can only see my photos if you're one of my close friends.

**S:** So have you posted more photos like this online?

**G:** Yes, I have! But, like I say, I don't let everyone see them. That could be dangerous!

### 2.2, p. 18, Ex 1

**I** = Interviewer, **L** = Laura

**I:** Why did you decide to become a doctor, Laura?

**L:** Well, I was always good at science subjects in school, and I really enjoyed them. I also used to work as an assistant to a paramedic in the summer. It was part of a volunteer project. I loved it... That's what convinced me to become a doctor.

**I:** Was studying medicine tough?

**L:** Yes, very. I had to do premed for six months, which involved classes, volunteer work and research, before applying to med school. Then I did four years of med school to get my degree, one year of social service, um, one year of residency and... four years of specialization in pediatrics.

**I:** Wow. That's more than ten years. And where did you do your social service?

**L:** They sent me to a small village in a remote region of Oaxaca. I was in charge of a small clinic. The culture was completely different from the city. I wasn't used to living in such a small community where everyone knows everyone else. I mean, I'm from one of the biggest cities in the world!

**I:** I imagine there was a lot to get used to! What other differences were there?

**L:** Well, when people were sick, they often went to a *curandero*, or traditional healer. Occasionally, they would come to the clinic for medication or bandages for a cut or sprain or something. But for many illnesses they were content to see the curandero.

**I:** And were the curanderos successful in treating people?

**L:** Most of the time I think they were... They have excellent knowledge of herbal medicine and massage. Pregnant women often go to a traditional midwife to give birth, sometimes in an adobe sauna, a *temascal*. They also do ritual cleansings with herbs and eggs or other objects. You know, I don't object to traditional medicine, I think it works well in many cases. Curanderos play an important role in rural areas. They're highly respected and trusted members of the community.

**I:** What about your job now?

**L:** Well, I have my practice as a pediatrician, and I work as a pediatric surgeon in the National Children's Hospital in Mexico City. I normally operate three mornings a week and the rest of the time I see patients in my office.

**I:** Have there been any recent changes in medicine that affect your job?

**L:** Oh yes, patients have much more access to medical information via the Internet. Self-diagnosis and self-medication are more common than they used to be. Now many parents bring their children in, and they've already checked the symptoms online and made a diagnosis. They know the entire contents of the relevant Wikipedia article! Sometimes I project an X-ray on the wall, and they start doing their own assessment of their child's illness! In the beginning it was frustrating, but now I'm getting used to it. Doctors are more used to dealing with this situation these days.

**I:** Finally, what do you like best and least about being a doctor?

**L:** I love operating and treating patients and seeing them in the children's ward getting better. I used to hate all the paperwork, but now I have an assistant to help me!

### 3.9, p. 33, Ex 2a

**A** = Ayaka, **L** = Laura

**A:** Hello?

**L:** Hi, it's Laura!

**A:** Laura? Good to hear from you. How are you?

**L:** I'm fine thanks. Very busy with the new job and everything... But what about you? How's life in New York?

**A:** It's OK. But to be honest, it's been very tough adapting to life here. I'm not used to living in such a big city.

**L:** I know, it's a big change for you! So, what are you finding most difficult?

**A:** Well, I just feel really lonely. I don't know anyone here... and it's really difficult to meet people and make friends.

**L:** I'm sorry to hear that. But what about work? What are your coworkers like? Is there anyone nice?

**A:** Yes, they're all really nice, but they have their own lives outside work. We sometimes go out for a drink on Fridays, but that still means I spend the whole weekend alone.

**L:** Oh no, that must be really hard on you. What about interests? Are there any classes you can take or anything?

**A:** Well, I go to a yoga class once a week and, I've finally taken up salsa dancing!

**L:** That's fantastic! So have you met anyone in the classes?

**A:** Not really. I don't want to sound negative, but... no one really speaks to me. And when I try talking to people, they're perfectly nice and everything, but they don't seem to want to have a conversation.

**L:** That sounds really difficult. I'm sure it'll get easier over time, though. If you see the same people every week, you'll soon get to know some of them.

**A:** Yes, you're probably right, it's just a question of time. But that's not all! The worst thing is, my apartment was robbed last week while I was at work!

**L:** Oh no, what did they take?

**A:** My TV and some jewelry—it wasn't valuable, but it had, you know, sentimental value.

**L:** Of course! You must feel terrible.

**A:** It was horrible... and now I feel really nervous being alone in the apartment.

**L:** Oh, you poor thing, you *are* having a bad time! Did you report it?
**A:** Yes, of course. The police were really helpful, and I've had the locks changed now. The good thing is, I have some really nice neighbors, and they've been very helpful and supportive.
**L:** You did the right thing, Ayaka! And knowing the neighbors is always a good thing. It's always difficult at first when you move to a new city but things will get better soon—I promise!
**A:** I know. I'm sorry to complain so much... but it's good to have someone to talk to.
**L:** Don't worry about it, I completely understand! I'm always here for you. And remember, I'm coming to see you soon. So start organizing a fun weekend, OK?
**A:** Sure. I'll get started right away!

### 5.6, *p. 56, Ex 1b*

**J** = Jessica, **P** = Panya

**J:** So, Panya, you're going to show me how to make a traditional Egyptian breakfast.
**P:** That's right, Jessica. It's called *ful medames*. It's an ancient Egyptian dish, nearly a thousand years old, but it's still a really popular breakfast in Egypt!
**J:** So how's it made?
**P:** Well, it can take a really long time to prepare—mostly because you need to soak and simmer the fava beans.
**J:** Fava beans?
**P:** That's right—the main ingredient! So first you need to soak the beans in water for eight to ten hours.
**J:** OK. That's a long time!
**P:** I know! Then you drain the beans and put them in a large pan. Next add some tomatoes, onion and garlic. Does that make sense?
**J:** Sorry, could you just say that again?
**P:** Of course, add some tomatoes, onion and garlic to the beans. Then cover the mixture with water and bring it to a boil. You need to be careful it doesn't boil over, though. Then turn the heat down and leave the ingredients to simmer overnight.
**J:** When you say "overnight," do you mean for *another* ten hours?
**P:** That's right!
**J:** That is a very long preparation time. So am I right in thinking you've already prepared these beans?
**P:** Yes, this is the bean mixture I cooked last night.
**J:** And is that the only way of doing it?
**P:** Well, you could use canned beans, but that'd be cheating!
**J:** OK, so what happens next?
**P:** Next you mash the mixture with a spoon, like this, to make it soft. Do you see what I mean? Do you want to go on mashing it?
**J:** Sure.
**P:** And once the beans are soft, you can stir in some salt and lemon juice. Are you following?
**J:** Mm, I think so. Can I just check something? Are there any spices in it?
**P:** Oh, yes, there are. I also added a little cumin before I mashed the beans.
**J:** Cumin, of course, that's what I can smell.
**P:** Next you grill some Egyptian flatbread to serve it with.
**J:** What exactly do you mean by "flatbread"?
**P:** It's just a kind of simple, thin bread.
**J:** Oh yes, of course. And is it served with anything else?
**P:** Yes, you can serve it with boiled or fried eggs. Today I'm going to fry some eggs in a little olive oil.
**J:** Mmm, delicious.
**P:** And finally, you serve the bean mixture warm with the bread and the eggs.
**J:** Mmm, it looks and smells delicious. But one thing I don't understand is why you make such a big, spicy meal for breakfast.
**P:** Ah. Well, you must remember that during the Muslim festival of Ramadan, people don't eat during the day, they fast. So, it makes sense to have a really big breakfast.

### 5.9, *p. 57, Ex 2a*

**A:** You know, Dorota, I've never had Polish food before...
**B:** Oh, it's delicious, you'll love it! Typical dishes use lots of cabbage, meat and cream.
**A:** Mmm. I don't understand anything on the menu, though.
**B:** Don't worry, I'll explain it. Well, we usually start with soup. There are two here. I'd recommend the *barszcz*– beetroot soup. It's really popular in Eastern Europe.
**A:** Hmm... what does it taste like?
**B:** It's delicious. As well as beetroot, it has other things... like onions and garlic in it, and vinegar, which gives it a sour flavor.
**A:** Hmm...
**B:** But if you're not sure, you could have the *zurek*. It's a white sausage and potato soup. It comes with a boiled egg in it. And most importantly, it's usually served in a bowl made of traditional Polish bread! It takes a long time to prepare!
**A:** Mmm, that sounds interesting. I'll have *zurek*, then.
**B:** OK, and I think I'll have the *barszcz*. And for the main course, I'd really recommend *golabki*.
**A:** *Golabki*? What's that?
**B:** It's very typical. It's cabbage stuffed with ground meat—pork and beef—and rice. It's baked in tomato sauce and served with sour cream.
**A:** That sounds nice, I'll definitely try that... Mmm, that was absolutely delicious! So, what about a dessert? I still have room! What are typical Polish desserts?
**B:** Well, we have lots of different cakes. *Makowiec* is the most typical and tasty Polish dessert.
**A:** What's it made with?
**B:** It's a kind of sweet bread made with poppy seeds. It also has almonds, raisins and honey in it. Ideally it shouldn't taste too sweet.
**A:** Should we try that then?
**B:** Yeah, let's!
**A:** And what are *kawa* and *herbata?*
**B:** Coffee and tea!
**A:** I'll have coffee... *kawa*!
**B:** Good. You're learning some Polish already!

### 6.1, *p. 59, Ex 3a*

**Karen**

I really like street performers. You know, musicians, mime artists and even those artists who draw pictures on the sidewalk. I like listening to street musicians as well, especially on the subway. Some of them are really good. It's really uplifting to hear live music on the way to work!

**Kinuko**

I like all sorts of entertainment, but I don't really like circuses. They're very depressing. I think it's cruel to keep wild animals in those conditions, and it's humiliating for them to do all those tricks! I guess circus performers are very talented, though.

**Shane**

When I went to Thailand last year, I saw a traditional puppet play called the *Hun Lakhon Lek*. It was amazing! The puppets were all about a meter tall, and each one had three puppeteers to move it. The puppeteers are also classical dancers, so the way the puppets move is really elegant and realistic.

**Vishal**

I love the movies! My favorite director is probably Quentin Tarantino. His movies are always action-packed, and the special effects are usually amazing! His latest script is for a Western and I can't wait to see that. I also really like Indian movies a lot. I mean, the plots can be a little predictable, but they always have a big cast so they're really visually interesting.

**Julie**

I really like stand-up comedy. I love how comedians think about everyday things in such random and unusual ways—they're hilarious! But if you go to a live show, don't sit next to the stage; the comedians always make you the focus of their jokes, and that can be pretty embarrassing!

**Helmut**

There's nothing like the atmosphere in a theater when the curtain goes up and you see the stage and scenery for the first time. It's like being transported to a different world! And I think a really good performance is much more moving and emotional than watching a movie. I love the energy between the performers and the audience.

# AMERICAN BIG PICTURE

## B2 [UPPER INTERMEDIATE] Split Edition a

Workbook

ALASTAIR LANE

Richmond
www.americanbigpicture.net

Richmond

58 St Aldates
Oxford
OX1 1ST
United Kingdom

Printed in Mexico

First edition: October 2012


**Publisher:** Deborah Tricker
**Content Development:** Eleanor Clements, Sarah Thorpe
**Editor:** Emily Binner
**Audio Production:** Motivation Sound Studios

**Cover Design:** Pentacor Book Design, Lorna Heaslip
**Design & Layout:** Lorna Heaslip, Dave Kuzmicki
**Picture Editor:** Helen Reilly/Arnos Design Ltd
**Art Coordinator:** Dave Kuzmicki
**Illustrators:** Francis Blake c/o Three-in-a-Box Ltd., page 24; Myles Talbot, page 73; Ron Wilson, page 29

**Photos:**
Arnos Design Ltd/David Oakley; Erden Eruc; Guardian News & Media Ltd 2011; Penguin Books Ltd; Maria Sanclement,; South West News Service/ Blake Ezra Cole/MASONS; TouchTunes Interactive Networks. ALAMY/Gunter Marx/EV, Big Cheese Photo LLC, Tomas de Arno, Jef Maion, Yu Liang Wong, Richard Levine, Jonathan Pearson, Chris Wilson, Photos12, Apex News and Pictures Agency, Ria Novosti, Outdoor-Archiv, Allesalltag, SHOUT, AF Archive, Fancy, Chuck Franklin, Ed Bock/Corbis Flirt, ITAR-ITASS Photo Agency, incamerastock, Catherine Paffey, TongRo Image Stock, The Art Archive, Steve Hamblin, Alamy Celebrity, Image Media Partners Ltd/Impact Photos, Sornos Images; CORDON PRESS; CORBIS/Hiep Vu/First Light, Matthew Wakem, Aurora Photos, Mallet/ Photocuisine, David Trilling, Image Source, Rainer Holz; FOTOLIA/ biker3, Antonio Oquias, Sergent, Misha, Paul Fleet; GETTY IMAGES Tom Kitchen, Tao Associates, Yellow Dog Productions, David Malan, Digital Vision, Frank Siteman, Jenifer Thermes, Alexander Nemeneov, Jupiter Images, Gary Yeowell, Photographer's Choice, Mark Lewis, Juice Images, Lounge Park, 2004 CBS Photo Archive, Simon Bruty, Adam Pretty, Lanny Ziering, Gray Mortimore, Photodisc, Bellurget Jean Louis, Amama Images, Stocktrek Images; GETTY IMAGES SALES SPAIN/Thinkstock; ISTOCKPHOTO/nkbimages, mattjeacock, Franco di Meo, denituvel, fonikum; PA PHOTOS/David Longstreath, Jose Acosta; ISTOCKPHOTO/ Getty Images Sales Spain; REUTERS/Attila Cser; REX FEATURES LTD/ Tom Campbell/Splashdown Direct, Lyndon Mechielsen/Newspix; THINKSTOCK/Istockphoto, George Doyle, Dynamic Graphics, Polka Dot, David de Lossy, Hemera, Creatas, Zoonar, Bananastock, Photos.com, Comstock; Albert Velasco; ARCHIVO SANTILLANA. © THINKSTOCK: Ablestock.com p. 9.

**Cover Photo:**
Big Apple at sunset, Fotolia © dell #9950038

**We would like to thank the following reviewers for their valuable feedback which has made *American Big Picture* possible. We extend our thanks to the many teachers and students not mentioned here.**

(Argentina): Cecilia Chiacchio, Ingrid Suhring; (Brazil): Ana Falcao, Virginia Garcia, Patricia McKay, Cynthia Phillipps, Bia Sousa; (Colombia): Kathleen Canal; (Italy): Morgan Cox, Karen Geiger, Sarah Stats; (Mexico): Emma Dominguez, Melissa Ferrin, Lupita Neve, Coral Ibarra Yunez; (Poland): Malgosia Adams, Marta Rosinska; (Spain): Vicki Anderson, Juan Carlos Araujo, Karen Dyer, Gabby Maguire, Fiona McClelland, Karin Rickatson, Almudena Verdugo Valcarce, Andy Walsh; (UK): Cathy Ellis, Howard Smith, Jonathan Stoddart

The Publisher has made every effort to trace the owner of copyright material; however, the Publisher will correct any involuntary omission at the earliest opportunity.

This book was printed in

# Contents


1 Social Networks page 2

2 Experts page 8

3 Survival page 14

Progress Test 1, Units 1–3 page 20

4 Reinvention page 22

5 Food for Thought page 28

6 That's Entertainment page 34

Progress Test 2, Units 4–6 page 40

Transcripts page 82

Track Listing

Irregular Verbs

# 1 SOCIAL NETWORKS

## VOCABULARY
### Relationships

**1** Read the clues and complete the puzzle. What is the hidden word in gray? ________________

1 Someone who tells you what to do in your job.
2 You play sports on the same side as this person.
3 Your mother or your father.
4 Someone you are in a business or romantic relationship with.
5 Someone who you know fairly well but who is not really a friend yet.
6 Someone traveling in a vehicle who is not driving.
7 Someone who works with you.
8 Someone you know well and get along with.

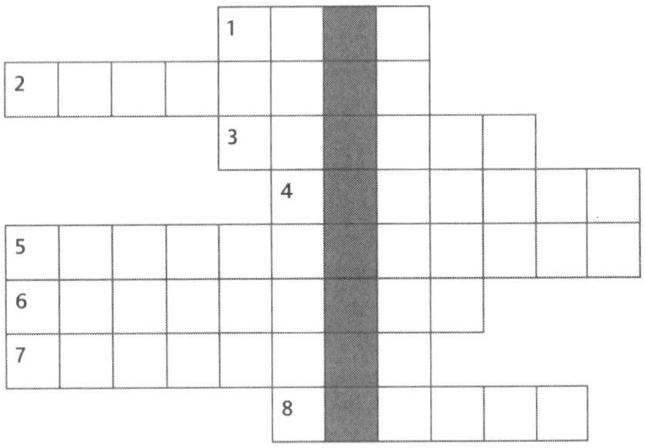


**2** Complete the words.

1 Cassandra is my m _ _ ag _ _ at work. She tells me what work to do.
2 My wife's mom and dad are really nice. It's great when you get along with your p _ r _ _ _ s- _ n-l _ _ .
3 I have three really c _ _ _ _ friends, and we spend all our time together.
4 I can't afford to rent an apartment by myself, so I need to find a r _ _ _ m _ _ e.
5 Meg is my b _ _ _ friend—we're almost like sisters!
6 I'm really enjoying my Chinese classes. My c _ _ s _ m _ t _ s are lots of fun!
7 Laura and Karl have been going out for about two months. They make a great c _ _ p _ _ !
8 I got lost on the way to the party, so I had to ask a p _ _ _ _ r _ _ for directions.

**3** Complete the sentences with the expressions from the box. There is one word you don't need.

| coworkers | ex-boyfriend | parents | parents-in-law |
|---|---|---|---|
| passerby | strangers | teammate | |

1 Your ____________ will have very similar DNA to you.
2 I get along well with my ________________ —we're still friends, even though we broke up last year.
3 I didn't meet my ________________ —my husband's mom and dad—until our wedding day.
4 While I was shopping this morning, a ____________ stopped me and asked me where I had bought my T-shirt!
5 Alba made some good friends in her last job. Her ____________ were a lot of fun.
6 I find it difficult to talk to ____________ . I never know what to say when I meet people for the first time.

**4** Match 1–6 to a–f to make complete sentences.

1 If you want Sara to be your girlfriend, you should ___
2 It was a real surprise. I was in the supermarket when I ___
3 Julie and Tim had a big argument and they ___
4 Nick and Vince are so annoying—they never ___
5 My new classmates are great. I ___
6 After the game today, the whole team is going to ___

a get along with them really well.
b show up on time.
c meet up at the café.
d broke up.
e ask her out.
f ran into my old English teacher.

### Phrasal verbs

**5** Choose the correct option to complete the sentences.

1 You're crazy to *drop / leave* out of school when you're only 17! You need to finish your studies!
2 Dimitri is going to travel around the world by himself. I know he can *take care / protect* of himself, but I still worry!
3 I wasn't playing any sports, so I *made / took* up running. I really enjoy it now.
4 I don't understand why you and Ximena are arguing. You should *do / make* up and be friends again.
5 Don't worry about our project. You can *count / number* on me to do my part of the work.
6 We've had a lot of difficulties in our relationship recently, but we've *spoken / talked* things over, and everything's OK now.
7 It's Marc's birthday on Sunday, so we're going to *go / stay* away to Boston for the weekend.
8 On weekends I usually *fly / hang* out with my friends at the mall.

## Vocabulary Extension
### Further phrasal verbs

**6** **a** 1.1 Listen to two speakers. Who says phrasal verbs a–j, speaker 1 or speaker 2?

a ☐ break down
b ☐ carry on
c ☐ give up
d ☐ go off
e ☐ turn in
f ☐ pick up
g ☐ set off
h ☐ straighten out
i ☐ throw away
j ☐ write down

**b** Match the speakers to the photos.

a ☐

b ☐

**7** Listen again. Complete the sentences.

1. We ______ ______ really early in the morning.
2. We ______ ______ my cousin at her house.
3. Suddenly, the car ______ ______ ! It just stopped right in the middle of nowhere!
4. Dad thought he could ______ the problem ______ , but it was too difficult for him to fix.
5. So we just ______ ______ and went home.
6. We were under a lot of pressure because we had to ______ ______ a big project later that day.
7. Suddenly, the fire alarm ______ ______ .
8. The university tests the fire alarms at 3 p.m. every Wednesday, so we ______ ______ working as usual.
9. I was just ______ ______ the last part of the report.
10. Apparently, someone ______ a cigarette ______ while it was still lit.

**8** Complete the sentences with the correct form of phrasal verbs from **6a**.

1. They're going on a three-day hike in the mountains. They*'re setting off* early tomorrow morning.
2. What day do we have to ______ the geography homework ______ to the teacher?
3. My roommate's alarm clock ______ at 6 a.m. every morning, and it always wakes me up!
4. Tell me what time your bus arrives, and I will ______ you ______ in my car.
5. It started raining in the middle of the soccer game, but my teammates wanted to ______ with the game, so by the end we were all really cold and wet.
6. The bus ______ on the way to school, so we had to get off and walk!
7. Don't ______ the newspaper ______ —I haven't read it yet!
8. Alberto started doing the Sudoku, but he ______ because it was too difficult!
9. ______ the e-mail address ______ on a piece of paper so you don't forget it.
10. Look at these books! There are hundreds of them. We'll need hours to ______ ______ the bookshelves.

## Bring It Together

**9** Complete the e-mail with one word in each blank.

Hi Martina,

I'm writing because I need some help! This week I had a meeting with my boss and my (1) ______ .
They told me that I was in big trouble for using the Internet too much during office hours. It was because I went to my sister's wedding last week and my new brother-in-law asked me to post the photos online. I don't have time at home, so I did it at work. Unfortunately, I don't get (2) ______ well with one of my coworkers. He saw me using the Internet, and he told everyone that I wasn't working! It's really unfair. I mean, he never turns his work (3) ______ on time, but I don't say anything about that!

Anyway, here's why I need your help. There's one really great photo of both my (4) ______ —my mom and dad look really nice in it. But it was taken on the street, and at the back of the picture there's a (5) ______ who is looking at the camera. I want to remove him from the picture, but I don't know how to do it. Can you straighten it (6) ______ for me? It's too difficult for me, and it's the last photo for the website. Please help! You know you're my (7) ______ friend in the world!

Thanks!

Love,

Elisa

## GRAMMAR
### Auxiliary verbs

**1** Complete the short answers.

1 A Are you on Facebook?
B Yes, we ______ .

2 A Have you changed your profile photo?
B No, I ______ .

3 A Will you please talk this over with Marie?
B No, I ______ .

4 A Does Kim use Twitter a lot?
B Yes, she ______ .

5 A Am I in that photo?
B No, you ______ .

6 A Did they meet up at the movie theater last night?
B No, they ______ .

**2** **a** Put the words and phrases in the correct order to make questions.

1 your who best is friend
______

2 get along you with boss do your
______

3 meet up did who you at the restaurant with
______

4 is what favorite your website
______

5 online you how often post do photos
______

**b** Answer the questions in **2a**.

1 ______
2 ______
3 ______
4 ______
5 ______

**3** Correct the sentences. Mark (✓) two correct sentences.

1 We're meeting up at the station, aren't?
2 Janice gets along well with her teammates, don't she?
3 Curtis and Todd didn't show up for class, did they?
4 You've invited your roommates, have you?
5 Dan's dropped out of college, isn't he?
6 You like Jane, don't you?
7 Farah and Tom aren't close friends, aren't they?
8 Nina has two roommates, she doesn't?

**4** Complete the online interview with one word in each blank (*isn't*, etc. = one word).

**Today's online chat is with technology expert Lupe Valdez. Join us live from 3 p.m.**

I Lupe, hi! So, your latest research project examines the way people use the Internet. Can you tell us more?

L Hi! Yes, I really (1) ______ believe the way we surf the Internet is changing.

I (2) ______ happening?

L Well, originally, people only went online using PCs. Now, many people visit websites using portable devices like cell phones or tablet.

I Yes, that's really changed things, (3) ______ it?

L Absolutely. It's partly because we now use apps to go online. This means we browse less—we visit the same web pages again and again.

I That's true. I (4) ______ spend less time browsing now that I have an iPhone! I use a lot of apps.

L Well, apps are fun, (5) ______ they? And very useful!

I Definitely. And they (6) ______ do some amazing things. Have you seen Layar?

L No, I (7) ______ .

I It's great. You can take a photo of a restaurant with your phone, then the app gives you reviews of it.

L Cool. I like Bump. You just touch iPhones with someone, and then you can share Facebook friends and other information.

I Sounds great! So what is your conclusion, Lupe?

L Well, the way we surf the Internet is changing. People are exploring less because they just use apps to visit the websites they like. I still (8) ______ know if that's a good thing or a bad thing.

I OK, thanks. Now readers, what do you think? Post your comments below.

## Past participles

**5** Complete the blog post with the correct form of the words from the box. There are two words that you don't need.

be create design feel finish
meet speak take tell write

**6** **a** Match 1–5 to a–e to make complete sentences.

1 I'm going to the beauty salon to ____
2 He called the police because he ____
3 When women get married, they often ____
4 We live on the sixteenth floor, so we ____
5 The customs officers stopped her, and she ____

a have a dress made for them.
b had his car stolen.
c had her bag searched.
d have our windows cleaned by professionals.
e have my hair cut.

**b** Which sentences describe

i a service that someone does for you?

____________

ii a bad experience that might happen to you?

____________

## Reflexive pronouns

**7** Complete the sentences with the correct reflexive pronouns.

1 Simon hurt ____________ when he was playing tennis.
2 Richard, you can help ____________ to anything from the refrigerator.
3 I looked at ____________ in the mirror.
4 Janet and Marina introduced ____________ to their new colleagues.
5 We taught ____________ to speak French from a book.
6 Sally's 14, so she's old enough to take care of ____________ .
7 Ask visitors to get ____________ a cup of tea or coffee when they arrive.
8 Girls, don't blame ____________ for the accident.

### New website!

OK, I know I've (1)____________ a lot of posts about this, but it's finally complete! The new website is (2)____________ and it looks fantastic. I think it will make a really big difference to the company. People had (3)____________ me that the old website was difficult to use, but for a long time I didn't listen. I had (4)____________ it myself and I felt proud of my work! But now I'm very glad I did something about it. The new site is totally different: it was (5)____________ by a web designer, and the photos were (6)____________ by a professional photographer, not just my friends! So far, the feedback has (7)____________ really positive—everyone I have (8)____________ to loves the new design. I'd love to know what you think, too—post your comments below!

Posted today at 9.36 a.m.

## BRING IT TOGETHER

**8** Read the article about a social networking site. Correct the words and phrases in bold. One word is already correct.

### Travel Buddies

Imagine you want to travel around the world or spend the summer in Europe, but none of your friends has the time or the money to go with you. No one likes spending all day alone, (1)**don't they**? If you don't want to travel around by (2)**itself**, why not find a friend on one of the best social networking sites around: travbuddy.com? The site (3)**designed** to help you find a travel companion. Users post their interests and explain where they want to go. It (4)**is become** a huge Internet success story, and the site (5)**was award** a Webby (the Oscars of the Internet) in 2010. We used the site (6)**themselves** last year during a trip to Indonesia. We met a local guy, and he showed us some cool places in his country. He also helped us out a lot when we (7)**made** our flights canceled on the last day. Of course, as with any website, you have to be very careful about meeting strangers: always go with a friend and meet new people in a (8)**crowded** area. One other possibility is to go to one of the Travbuddy unofficial get-togethers. Users of the site (9)**have hold** these in lots of different places, and they're a great way to meet people. I wanted to set one up in my hometown last year, but then I discovered another person (10)**was already organized** one. So I went along and met some new friends for my next trip... to Mexico!

## FUNCTIONAL LANGUAGE Small talk

**1** Complete the words.

1 At the airport

A Hi, Luis, and welcome to Seattle!

B Thanks, Julie. Nice to meet you at last. Wow, it's really warm today, (1)i_______ it?

A Yeah, it is. I think you've (2)b_______ the hot weather with you from Brazil!

B That's true. It's really hot back home at the moment.

A I went to Brazil once. I was in Salvador for the carnival. It's amazing, isn't it?

B I love Salvador, but I'm not really a big (3)f_______ of the carnival to be (4)h_______ .

A Really? I loved it!

2 At a training course

C So, Daniel, your boss works in Panama, (5)d_______ she? She's the lady with long, dark hair?

D No, my boss is Carlos Gutierrez. As a matter of fact, he's here today.

C Oh, sorry, I must be thinking of someone (6)e_______ .

D It's an easy mistake to make. It's a big company. We sell computers all over the world.

C (7)S_______ of computers, should we find somewhere to check our e-mail?

D Sure. (8)W_______ you like to go to the cafeteria? They have free WiFi there.

C Sounds great!

## LISTENING Listening for gist

**1** **a** 1.2 Listen to two conversations. Match the conversations to two of the photos.

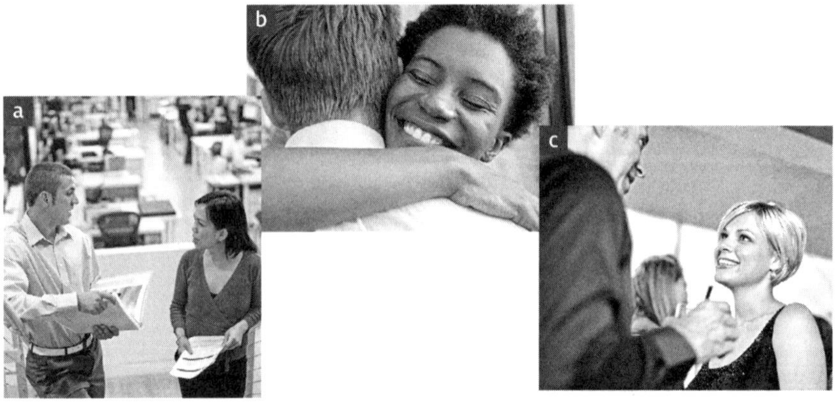

**b** In which conversation are the speakers meeting for the first time? ____________

**2** Listen again. Complete the sentences.

1 Vera is Julieta's ____________ .
2 There were ____________ students in Julieta's Spanish class.
3 Nick is from ____________ .
4 The temperature in Nick's hometown was ____________ degrees.
5 Paula has just arrived in ____________ .
6 Michaela is an ex____________ of Paula's.
7 Michaela has ____________ hair.
8 Michaela was studying ____________ .

**STRATEGY** The first time you hear an audio, listen for gist (the main idea). Then listen again more carefully for specific information.

## READING Activating background knowledge

**1** **a** Read the title of the text on page 7. Which of the words in the box would you expect to see in the article?

acquaintance
best friend boss
colleague coworker
passerby relationships
roommate stranger

**b** Read the article quickly. Mark (✓) the words in **1a** that appear in the article.

**2** Choose the correct option, a, b or c. Then read the text again to check your answers.

1 Robin Dunbar studied...
   a how teenagers make friends.
   b some people from very simple societies.
   c the work that people do in modern offices.
2 When they looked at Leila's Facebook friends, they looked at...
   a all her friends.
   b only her closest fifty friends.
   c fifty friends selected by chance.
3 They agreed that someone was a real friend of Leila if...
   a they frequently e-mailed or spoke to her.
   b they had been to school together.
   c they had a lot of acquaintances.
4 They believe that Leila has...
   a more real friends than Dunbar's Number.
   b exactly the same number of real friends as Dunbar's Number.
   c fewer real friends than Dunbar's Number.
5 One Facebook friend wasn't Leila's real friend because...
   a it was an animal.
   b he was a celebrity.
   c he was a fictional character.
6 Leila's college roommate...
   a has dropped out of school.
   b used to get along well with her.
   c gets together with her a lot.
7 The writer concludes that...
   a people have more friends because of sites like Facebook.
   b sites like Facebook have no effect at all on our relationships.
   c people use sites like Facebook because they don't like losing friends from the past.

**STRATEGY** Before you read a new text, look at the title. This will give you a clue to the content. Then try to think of words or vocabulary that you might expect to see in the article. This can help you understand the content right from the beginning.

# How Many Facebook Friends Do We Really Have?

Robin Dunbar of Oxford University believes that the human brain can only remember social groups of up to 150 people. He discovered "Dunbar's Number" (150) by studying everything from primitive tribes to coworkers in modern offices. But what of the younger generation?

One member of our team, Leila Brillson, has over 500 Facebook friends, and she volunteered herself for a small experiment. We wondered if Dunbar's Number would still be true in a Facebook world. What percentage of Leila's virtual friends really were her friends?

## The Rules

We chose fifty random friends and then asked Leila questions about them. Depending on the answers, we decided whether the person actually was Leila's friend, based on:

- regular involvement in her life
- strong emotional connection
- continuous effort to stay in touch

If the person didn't meet all those qualifications, they weren't a friend—just an acquaintance.

## The Data

Out of fifty random people, we decided that thirty-one were not Leila's friends, suggesting that 38% of the people on her Facebook are real friends. 190 friends (38% of 500) isn't far off from Dunbar's 150.

Leila knew most of her real friends not through high school but via a social circle, dating or work. Also, anyone that she is a fan of (e.g., a band) is counted by Facebook as a friend, and Leila is certainly not really friends with everyone on her list, like superstar singer Nick Cave.

We argued over three people:

1 College Roommate

Leila insisted that she and her college roommate were still good friends, even though they hadn't seen each other for about four years.

2 Coworker or Colleague

When explaining about a former colleague, Leila mentioned that they ran into each other all the time and speak every now and again. We decided this was not a friend, but rather a business contact.

3 Ex-best Friend

Despite having grown apart from a good friend in high school, Leila declared they were still friends because of, well, history. We refused this one because without Facebook, Leila would have no idea where this person was.

## Conclusions

Dunbar suggests that there is no "Facebook effect" and that social circles do not really expand because of Facebook. What is different though, is that people like Leila have a different definition of a friend to Dunbar. Leila was always hesitant to say someone wasn't a friend, especially when they once were. Here is the attraction of Facebook: it offers a world where relationships never stop. Sure, old acquaintances may be gone, but now they won't be forgotten.

# 2 EXPERTS

## VOCABULARY

### Health

**1** Circle the word that doesn't work in each sentence.

1 *An acupuncturist / A homeopath / A pharmacist* is an example of an expert in alternative medicine.
2 You need a *chiropractor / herbalist / specialist* to look at your back.
3 A *herbalist / pharmacist / surgeon* sells cures for various health problems.
4 My dad needed to see a well-known *acupuncturist / midwife / surgeon* to cure the pain in his neck.
5 My aunt works in the city hospital as a *shaman / nurse / surgeon*.

**2** Complete the patient–doctor conversations with the words from the box.

antibiotics infection injection
insomnia rash vaccination

1 P Can you give me some ___________ , doctor?
D No, they won't help you because you have a virus.

2 P Why did you want to see us, doctor?
D All the children in the school are getting a measles ___________, including your daughter.

3 D I'm sorry, but I have to give you an ___________ .
P Oh no! Will it be painful?

4 P I'm not sleeping well at the moment. I feel exhausted all the time!
D I'm sorry to hear that. I expect you have ___________ .

5 P I cut my foot, and then I went swimming and now look at it. The cut won't heal!
D Every time you cut yourself, you should wash the cut and cover it to prevent an ___________ .

6 P I started using the pills you prescribed, and now I have a ___________ on my arm. Look, it's all red.
D OK, I think we should change that medicine.

**3** Complete the words.

1 You get a b _ _ ka _ _ e because you have bad posture.
2 The most popular p _ _ nk _ l _ _ _ s are aspirin and paracetamol.
3 The surgeons performed a seven-hour heart o _ e _ a _ _ o _ .
4 I fell off my bike, and now I have a big black and blue b _ _ _ s _ on my elbow.
5 Can you buy me some cough s _ _ _ p if you go to the drugstore?
6 Oh dear, your forehead feels very hot. I think you might have a t _ _ p _ _ at _ _ _ .
7 I was hit by a golf ball, and now I have a b _ _ p on my head!

**4** Choose the correct options to complete the sentences.

1 Have you *taken / done* your medicine yet?
2 You need to *make / do* a doctor's appointment.
3 I think you have a fever. I'll *make / take* your temperature.
4 The doctor will *write / do* you a prescription.
5 Gina's gone to bed because she *did / felt* sick.
6 We can *take / treat* this illness with antibiotics.
7 Fatima's not well. She *got / took* a throat infection last weekend.
8 Oh dear, you *feel / have* all the symptoms of the flu.

### Medicine

**5** Complete the text with the words from the box.

bandage medication nurses paramedic
patients room surgeons wards

**I love my job because...**

***So what do you do, Lindsay?***
I'm a (1) ___________ —I work with the ambulance team at the local hospital.
***And is it a difficult job?***
That depends. It can be very stressful. Sometimes our work is just putting a (2) ___________ on a person's injury or giving them some (3) ___________ . At other times, we have to get someone to an operating (4) ___________ as quickly as possible, for example after an accident. It can be a matter of life and death.
***Of course. Do you spend time at the hospital, too?***
I rarely spend time in the hospital (5) ___________ , unless I am visiting someone we've helped. When we get to the hospital, our job is done. After that, we have to leave the (6) ___________ and other specialists to do what they can.
***And what's the best thing about your job?***
The people. I feel that I can make a difference to the lives of our (7) ___________ , which means a lot to me. The doctors and (8) ___________ at the hospital are great, too. I wouldn't change my job for anything in the world!

**6** Complete the *-ever* words.

1 A You failed your driving test again. Are you going to stop taking lessons?
B No! I am going to learn to drive ______ever many lessons it takes me!

2 A Is it OK if I sit here?
B Yes, sit ______ever you like. Make yourself at home.

3 A ______ever you do, don't tell Jim about the party!
B Don't worry, I won't tell him anything.

4 A I feel terrible! I don't know if it's the flu or just a cold.
B Well, I don't think you can go to work today ______ever you have.

5 A I'm asking all the teachers if they want to go on the school trip next Saturday.
B Well, ______ever decides to go needs to know about first aid.

6 A What time should I come to your house on Saturday?
B You can come ______ever you like. We'll be home all day.

## Vocabulary Extension

### Treatment

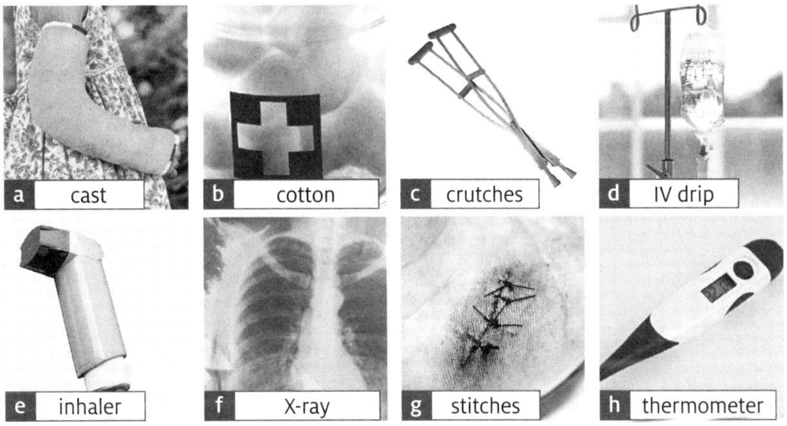


**7** Complete the sentences with the words from the photos.

1 Dana got hurt playing hockey, and she needed six ____________ in her forehead.
2 You're not allowed to drink anything before the operation, so we're going to put you on an ____________ .
3 The surgeon isn't sure what's wrong with your toe, so she wants to take an ____________ of your foot.
4 I have asthma, but it's OK. I just use my ____________ when I'm having breathing difficulties.
5 Use this ____________ to take your temperature.
6 Rosie broke her arm and it's in a ____________ —all her friends have written messages on it!
7 I can't walk without ____________ . My ankle hurts too much.
8 The nurse will get some ____________ to clean the blood off your knee.

## Bring It Together

**8** **Complete the text with the words from the box. There are two words that you don't need.**

appointment backaches Band-Aid diagnosis however patient prescription treat whatever whenever

### Acupuncture

Acupuncture began in ancient China where it was used to (1) ____________ a huge number of illnesses and diseases. Today it remains popular, although many doctors only recommend it for certain problems such as (2) ____________ .

So how does it work? During the (3) ____________ , the acupuncturist asks the (4) ____________ questions about his or her general health. Then the acupuncturist begins the treatment and may insert up to a dozen metal needles.

Acupuncture is a form of alternative medicine. So if you choose to try it, (5) ____________ you do, do not stop taking other medicines. If you have a (6) ____________ from your normal doctor, continue using it.

It is also best to get a clear (7) ____________ of your problem from a normal doctor. In some countries anyone can be an acupuncturist. So (8) ____________ you go to see one, make sure that they have proper qualifications from a professional organization.

# GRAMMAR
## The present

**1** Choose the correct options to complete the sentences.

1 The pharmacy *opens / is opening* at 8:30 a.m.
2 *I really hate / I'm really hating* injections. I'm scared of needles!
3 My father *is taking / takes* medication every day.
4 My nursing course *starts / is starting* next month.
5 *I often get / I'm often getting* colds in winter.
6 Jan *is taking / takes* antibiotics at the moment. He has an infection.
7 *I go / I'm going* to the pharmacy now to get my dad's prescription.
8 The surgeon *waits / is waiting* in the operating room.

**2** Match a–b to i–ii.

1 a My sister goes... ____
b Right now they're... ____
i running in the park.
ii running every day.

2 a I'm thinking... ____
b I think... ____
i about joining a gym.
ii gyms are a waste of money.

3 a This bruise feels... ____
b You're feeling... ____
i well again.
ii really painful.

4 a He's always hated... ____
b He hates ____
i going to the doctor.
ii his chemistry course.

5 a I'm always taking painkillers... ____
b I always take painkillers... ____
i because I have a bad back.
ii when I have a backache.

6 a He's trying... ____
b He has tried... ____
i taking diet pills.
ii to lose weight at the moment.

7 a I've done yoga... ____
b I do yoga... ____
i because it helps me relax.
ii since I was young.

**3** Complete the text with the correct form of the verbs in parentheses.

Home | About me | Links | Contact

### Pilates Blog

I'm Lola Puyol and I'm a Pilates instructor in Caracas. Welcome to my first ever blog! I (1)_________ (write) it to tell people about Pilates and my life.

So what is Pilates? It's a way of staying in shape. Millions of people (2)_________ (do) it worldwide every day. It (3)_________ (strengthen) your mind and body. Pilates students also (4)_________ (use) a lot of equipment. For example, in the picture, I (5)_________ (teach) one of my students how to use "the reformer." Alba, my student, (6)_________ (push) with her legs to build up the core muscles of the body. This is probably our most famous piece of equipment.

As for me, I (7)_________ (be) a Pilates teacher for eight years now, but there are still things I want to learn. For the next seven days, my friend Antonio and I (8)_________ (take) a course to become better teachers. It was Antonio's idea. He (9)_________ (think) that we should do it to improve our knowledge of all the techniques.

Pilates isn't just for fun, either. Some American scientists (10)_________ (study) Pilates at the moment to see if it can help patients with Parkinson's Disease. I'll tell you more about that next week.

Comments 0 posted Tuesday, March 29, 11:13 a.m.

**4** Correct the sentences. Mark (✓) two correct sentences.

1 I'm being a pharmacist for almost twenty years.
2 I'm not believing in alternative medicine.
3 Do you take any medicine at the moment?
4 Jean's going to the chiropractor every month.
5 You are needing a vaccination before going to Africa.
6 Chris has felt sick all week.
7 You're always catching colds!
8 I try to lose weight at the moment.

## Used to do/used to doing

**5** **a** Put the words in the correct order to make sentences.

1 used pills she to take diet

______________________________

2 not I'm to exercising used

______________________________

3 to use a personal didn't we have trainer

______________________________

4 taking medicine he's used to the getting

______________________________

5 in to can't used I get hospital being the

______________________________

**b** Which sentences in **5a** describe

i the past? ____________

ii the present? ____________

**6** Complete the sentences with one word in each blank (*don't*, etc. = one word).

*When I was younger, I* (1) ____________ *to be really out of shape. I didn't* (2) ____________ *to like walking—I drove everywhere! I felt tired all the time and I* (3) ____________ *to get a lot of headaches, but I didn't think there was anything wrong. I was* (4) ____________ *to feeling like that. Then my husband encouraged me to start exercising and, within just a few weeks, the headaches were gone! Now I'm much healthier. I go running about three mornings a week. At first I didn't enjoy getting up early, but I* (5) ____________ *used to it now—it's part of my routine. I'm also* (6) ____________ *used to eating a healthier diet. I* (7) ____________ *to buy a lot of ready meals, but now I cook more fresh food. I still don't like vegetables much, but I think I'll* (8) ____________ *used to them eventually!*

**7** Complete the sentences with the correct form of the words in parentheses and the correct form of *used to*.

1 ____________ (you/eat) a lot of junk food when you were young?

2 Nikos still doesn't like the gym, but now he has a personal trainer, he ____________ (go) there.

3 I'm not used to having backaches—I ____________ (not/get) them when I was younger.

4 My grandma ____________ (take) an aspirin every day. She's done it for years.

5 Lots of people find acupuncture strange at first, but they quickly ____________ (have) the treatment.

6 I'm a pediatrician, so I ____________ (not/work) with adults—I only treat children.

## BRING IT TOGETHER

**8** Choose the correct options to complete the messages from an advice website.

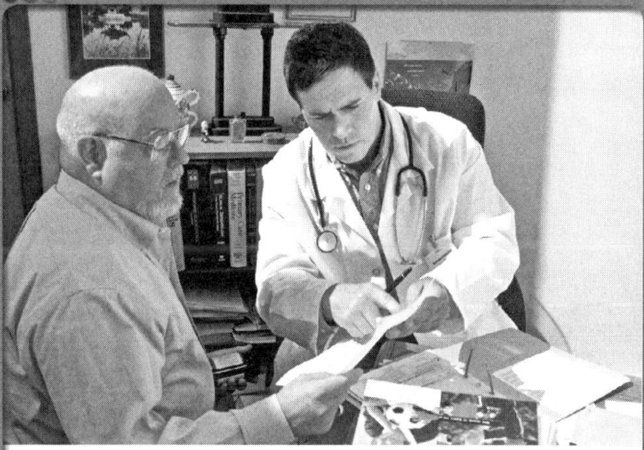

### Self-diagnosis?

At the moment, my husband (1)*suffers / is suffering* from a red rash on his leg. (2)*He has / He's had* the symptoms for a week now, and he doesn't seem to be getting better. Today he (3)*reads / was reading* about his symptoms online, and now he wants to do some self-medication! I'm worried because, in this country, pharmacists (4)*sell / are selling* many medicines without a prescription, including powerful drugs like antibiotics! What can I do?

AG

This isn't a new problem. Before modern hospitals, people (5)*use to / used to* invent their own cures for diseases, but that didn't mean the cures worked. Today, many people (6)*are / get* used to looking their symptoms up on the Internet when they feel sick. This is harmless if they look at websites by medical professionals. However, it cannot replace a visit to the doctor. Many people (7)*don't understand / aren't understanding* that certain symptoms have different causes. The last time I heard about someone with this problem, I advised her to bring her printouts to my office. That patient (8)*has now been / has now gotten* used to doing this and discusses the possible symptoms with her doctor. Maybe the same system could work for your husband, too.

MD

## FUNCTIONAL LANGUAGE
### Making polite requests

**1** 2.1 Listen to a conversation in a doctor's office. Complete the appointment card.

Patient name: *Jennifer Chan*

Appointment with: ____________

Date: ____________

Time: ____________

**2** **a** Complete the questions from the conversation in **1**.

1 I ____________ if you ____________ give me some advice.
2 ____________ you ____________ me if I need any vaccinations?
3 Would it be ____________ to get the vaccinations here in the clinic?
4 Do you ____________ any ____________ how long the appointment will take?
5 ____________ you ____________ writing that on a card for me?

**b** Listen again and check.

## LISTENING Choosing the correct option

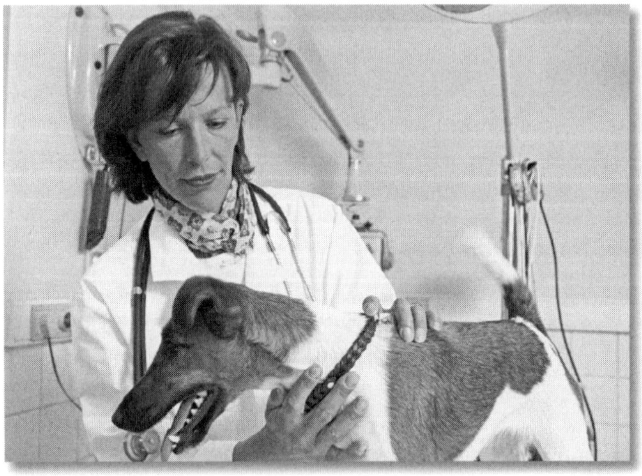

**1** 2.2 Listen to a radio program about training to become a vet. Number topics a–e in the order you hear about them.

a hands-on experience ____________
b disadvantages of being a vet ____________
c types of animal ____________
d school subjects ____________
e advice about college ____________

**2** **a** Choose the correct answers to the questions.

1 What kind of animals does Alexandra work with now?
  a farm animals
  b family pets
  c unusual animals
2 Which school subject is Gina best at?
  a biology
  b chemistry
  c math
3 Where is Gina working as a volunteer?
  a at an animal shelter
  b at a local farm
  c at a riding center
4 What warning does Alexandra give about working as a vet?
  a Vets get badly injured by the animals they work with.
  b Vets have to make difficult decisions.
  c Vets must work very long hours.
5 What should Gina do before starting college?
  a travel
  b get advice about financing
  c do a lot of studying

**b** Listen again and check.

**STRATEGY** When you have to answer multiple-choice questions, read the questions and options carefully. Remember that all the options may contain words from the audio. The first time you listen, try to identify the correct answers. The second time you listen, check your answers. Why are the other options wrong?

## WRITING Using facts & figures

**1** Read the blog post quickly and answer the questions.

1 What type of images are A–C?

2 Which countries do the data in A–C come from?

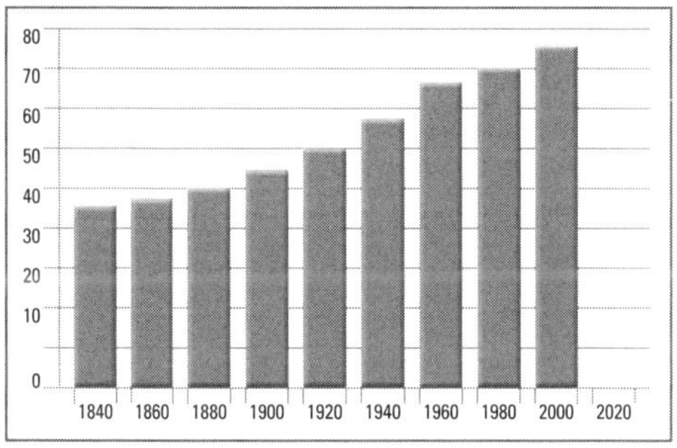


A

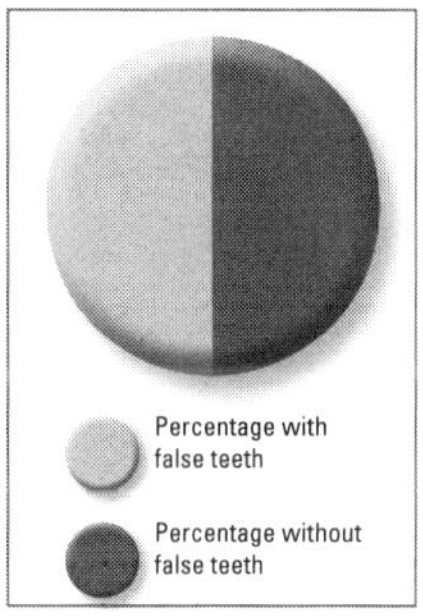


B

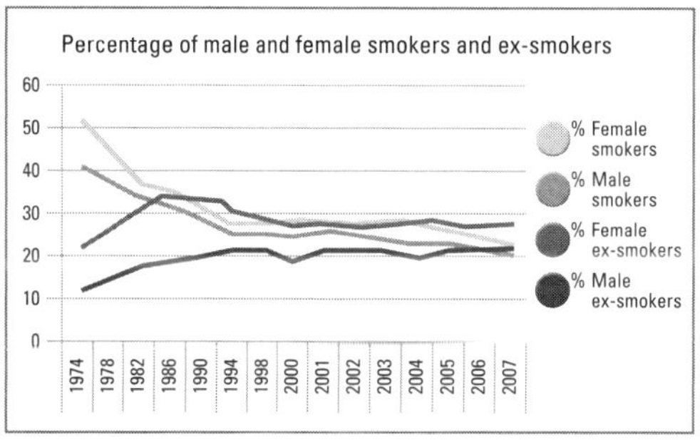


C

### The Good Old Days? – Rutger Van Sciver

This week there has been a whole series of TV shows about declining health in society. I disagree with them so strongly that I had to write about it. The good old days never happened! I'm going to look at some statistics from three different countries, but I think they show general trends. All these diagrams were sourced from the Internet.

First of all, if people were healthier in the past, why was life expectancy so low? Look at figure A, the bar graph for the USA. This reveals that in 1920, most people died before they were 50. A century ago, most people never met their grandparents. It can clearly be seen that life expectancy has risen year on year, even during depressions and wars.

People don't just live longer, they live better, too. Take diagram B, the pie chart from my country, the Netherlands. It tells us that back in 1981, roughly half of all people had false teeth. People didn't take care of themselves in the same way in the past, and things like toothpaste, mouthwash and dental floss were nowhere near as good as they are today. Nowadays the percentage of people with false teeth is less than 33%.

This brings me to my third visual aid, chart C. What this line graph demonstrates is that the number of smokers in the UK has fallen every year since 1974. This has an overall impact on the entire population. I was born in 1960, and I can remember in my childhood that cigarette smoke was everywhere—on buses, in movie theaters and even on planes. Now this has completely changed: it's another example of how people today take better care of their health. We live longer, cleaner and healthier lives. So how can people say that things were better in the past?

**2** Complete the sentences with the missing words. Check your answers in the blog post.

1 I'm going to look at some st _ _ _ s _ _ cs from three different countries, but I think they s _ _ _ general trends.

2 All these diagrams were s _ _ _ c _ d from the Internet.

3 Look at f _ g _ _ _ A, the bar graph for the USA. This r _ v _ _ _ s that...

4 It can c _ _ _ r _ y be seen that life expectancy has r _ _ _ n year on year.

5 Take d _ _ g _ _ m B, the pie chart from my country, the Netherlands. It t _ _ _ s us that back in 1981, over half of all people had false teeth.

6 Nowadays the p _ _ cent _ _ _ of people with false teeth is less than 33%.

7 What this line graph d _ m _ _ s _ r _ t _ s is that...

**3** Write a reply to Rutger's blog post. Do you agree or disagree with his argument? Refer to his diagrams or any others that you can find online.

**STRATEGY**

When we refer to charts or diagrams, we usually use the present simple tense and verbs like *reveal*, *show*, *tell*. We use the noun form to describe the data that they show, e.g., *the number of smokers*, *the percentage of people*. Notice that we say data is *in* the chart or *in* the diagram.

# 3 SURVIVAL

## VOCABULARY
### Equipment

**1 a** Complete the text with the words from the box.

compasses   life jackets   life rafts   rope
sails   waterproof clothing

It's one thing to travel across the ocean in a boat with (1)______ for wind power—but how about crossing the Pacific using only the strength of your arms? Turkey's Erden Eruç set out to do just that in 2007.
An ocean crossing is incredibly dangerous, and Eruç was careful to stay safe. On board, he had plenty of (2)______ to keep him dry, and he also had space for two (3)______ to replace his main boat if it sank! Eruç took two (4)______ to find North and two (5)______ to wear if he got thrown overboard. Falling into the ocean would be really dangerous so he also had a (6)______ tying his leg to the boat.
Unfortunately, even with these preparations, Eruç had to abandon his trip in May 2008 when the crossing became impossible. But in 2010, Eruç finally achieved his dream, and in doing so he became the first person to have rowed across three oceans—the Atlantic, the Indian and the Pacific.

**b** Match 1–6 to a–f.

1 Is that a boat over there? I can't see very well. ____
2 That's a bad cut on your leg. ____
3 We don't need a map. ____
4 There's no electricity, and it's really dark. ____
5 Don't forget to pack your thermal underwear! ____
6 Radar is very useful if you have to navigate in bad weather. ____

a There's a GPS in the car.
b You can use it to see where other boats are.
c Pass me the binoculars, please.
d Do you know where the flashlight is?
e That will keep you warm when you're in Canada.
f It's lucky there's a first-aid kit.

### Personality adjectives

**2** Complete the words.

1 You have to be very d __ t __ __ m __ n __ d to complete a marathon. It's a lot of hard work.
2 Vicky is very m __ tu __ __ for her age. She's 14, but she acts like an 18-year-old.
3 Our team is w __ __ l-p __ __ p __ __ ed for the expedition. We have bought all the equipment we need.
4 I think hikers who leave trash in the national park are completely ir __ __ __ p __ __ __ ib __ __ .
5 After the earthquake, many people were saved by the c __ __ r __ ge __ __ __ actions of firefighters, who were working in very dangerous conditions.
6 Carl is r __ __ k __ __ ss because he takes so many unnecessary risks.
7 Shin-cho is a very ex __ __ __ ie __ __ __ __ mountain climber. He's been to the Alps, the Andes and the Himalayas.
8 Dino is a very r __ s __ l __ __ nt tennis player. He very often has a difficult match but wins it in the end.
9 The boat has everything we need to survive at sea. We can be completely s __ l __ -s __ ff __ __ __ __ n __.
10 To drive across the desert, you need to be very r __ s __ u __ c __ f __ l. There will lots of problems, and you can't predict them.

### Talking about danger

**3** Correct the sentences. Mark (✓) two correct sentences.

1 If you don't take a compass, you're at danger of getting lost.
2 We got into trouble while we were kayaking and we had to call for help.
3 My friends go diving, but I just watch them safe from the boat!
4 Don't do risks when you're swimming in the ocean. Anything can happen.
5 Everything got wrong on the trip: the flight was delayed, the kids got sick, and the hotel was terrible.
6 I'm going to go backpacking around the world. I'm not care about the risks!
7 Our travel agency will take all the necessary precautions before we go white-water rafting.
8 We need to warn the tourists on pickpockets on the trains.

## Weather

**4** Read the clues and complete the puzzle. What is the hidden word in gray? ____________

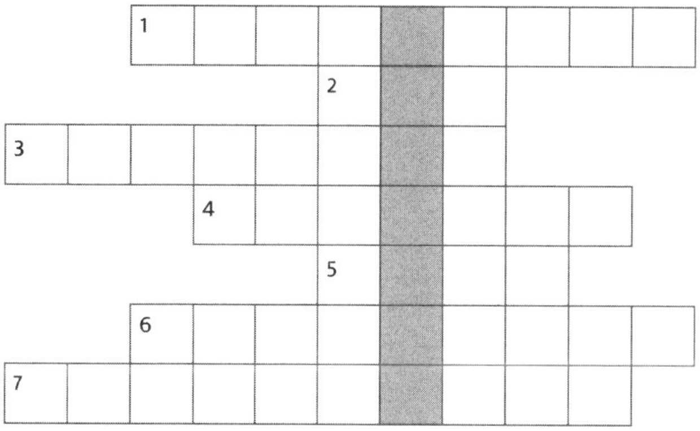

1 Bursts of very bright light that you see in a storm.
2 A thick cloud at ground level that makes it very difficult to see.
3 Strong winds and a lot of snowfall.
4 A loud noise you hear during a bad storm.
5 A very strong (e.g., 100 kilometer-per-hour) wind.
6 A pile of deep snow created by the wind.
7 Small balls of ice that fall from the sky.

## Vocabulary Extension

### Word building

**5** Complete the word chart.

| Verb | Noun | Adjective |
|---|---|---|
| (1) | (2) | (un)assisted |
| damage | (3) | (4) |
| isolate | (5) | (6) |
| injure | (7) | injured |
| recognize | (8) | (9) (un) |
| (10) | rescue / rescuer | |
| | severity | (11) |
| survive | (12) survival / | |

**6** **a** Complete the sentences with the correct form of six words from **5**.

1 After the tornado, the emergency services soon started searching for ____________ .
2 The storm caused a lot of ____________ to her boat, but she was able to sail to safety.
3 They managed to get out of the snowdrift with a little ____________ .
4 We feel very ____________ in the winter—the snow makes it hard for people to visit us.
5 It was a ____________ storm that affected large areas of the country.
6 His car was so badly damaged that it was ____________ .

**b** 3.1 Listen and check.

## Bring It Together

**7** Complete the text with the words from the box.

blizzard precautions radar reckless rescue risks snowdrifts survival waterproof clothing well-prepared

**avalanche** *(n)* /ˈævəlɑːntʃ/
a sudden fall of snow from a mountainside

### Safety in the Mountains

If you enjoy winter sports in the mountains, you need to be aware of the (1) ____________ involved so that you stay safe. If you are caught in a storm, you need to be wearing (2) ____________ so that you stay dry. It is a good idea to wear goggles, too. These can help if you are caught in a (3) ____________ ; without them, you can be blinded by the snow. Poles are useful, too, as bad weather can produce (4) ____________ , where snow is blown into a pile by the wind.

It is also important to be aware of the danger of avalanches. You need to check the weather conditions and find out about the terrain you are planning to cross. You also need to make sure you are (5) ____________ . For example, you should carry a device called an ARVA. This will enable others to (6) ____________ you if you are caught by an avalanche and buried under snow. Some people also use a gadget that uses (7) ____________ , like on ships. In an avalanche, you have a 50% chance of dying if you are buried for more than twenty minutes, so not carrying these devices is incredibly (8) ____________ . Your chances of (9) ____________ may depend on you and others in your party having one, so they are essential pieces of equipment.

You can enjoy doing winter sports safely if you take sensible (10) ____________ before you go into the mountains and while you are there.

## GRAMMAR
### Narrative tenses

**1** Complete the sentences with one word in each blank (*don't*, etc. = one word).

1 There was a bad storm yesterday, so we ______ go sailing.
2 What ______ you doing when the storm started?
3 They ______ heard the news before I called them. It was a shock for them!
4 He was exhausted because he'd ______ climbing all day.
5 When the boat began to sink, many passengers jumped into the water and ______ to the shore.
6 We were very tired because we ______ been walking in the snow for hours.
7 Last night, Cathy steered the boat while I ______ sleeping.
8 ______ anyone checked the weather forecast before you started the expedition?

**2** Choose the correct options to complete the sentences.

1 When I looked through the binoculars, I *saw / was seeing* the island.
2 When they were rescued, they *had spent / were spending* three weeks underground.
3 Mom called us while we *had traveled / were traveling* on the train.
4 They were incredibly relieved to see another ship. They *sat / had been sitting* in the life raft for three days.
5 I didn't want to disturb Don because he *studied / was studying* the map.
6 When we were at sea, we realized we *hadn't packed / weren't packing* the first-aid kit.
7 The forest fire *had burned / had been burning* for two hours before the firefighters arrived to put it out.
8 They checked the life rafts. They *set / were setting* the GPS, and then they left.
9 After I got into the dive cage, I realized that I *hadn't charged / had been charging* my camera battery.
10 We arrived at the airport just as check-in *was closing / had been closing*, so we were able to get on the plane.

**3** Use the words to write sentences in the past.

1 I feel tired because I run
*I felt tired because I had been running.*
2 Rita meet her boyfriend when they travel on a bus
______
3 Elena not go rock climbing last weekend because she hurt her arm
______
4 the girls see an eagle when they camp in the woods
______
5 we need a break because we drive for hours
______
6 while Alfonso drive to his girlfriend's house a hailstorm suddenly hit
______

**4** Complete the text with the past continuous, past perfect or past perfect continuous form of the verbs in parentheses.

**Shipwrecked on Mogmog**

The island of Mogmog is one of the most remote places on Earth, and for the next six months it will be home to the Barrie family from Australia. Last month, the Barries (1) ______ (sail) across the Pacific when they were caught in a storm. While hurricane-force winds (2) ______ (blow) across their boat, they decided to head for the safety of Mogmog. Unfortunately, their boat was damaged when it (3) ______ (approach) the beach. It hit some metal that American soldiers (4) ______ (leave) there sixty years ago. Fortunately, the islanders helped them bring the boat ashore, although one man injured his hand when they (5) ______ (take) it out of the water.

Although the family was delighted to be safe, they soon realized their boat needed serious repairs. After Mr. Barrie (6) ______ (speak) to experts back home, he discovered that they needed six months to complete them. Fortunately, the islanders have made their guests very welcome. The Barries' daughters were especially pleased to meet the local children after they (7) ______ (spend) months at sea. Now they spend their time playing on the beach, but it's not all fun in the sun. Before the accident, they (8) ______ (study) online with a teacher in Australia, and once they arrived on Mogmog, their lessons started again!

## Adverbs

**5** **a** Complete the sentences with the adverb form of the word in parentheses.

1 *Happily,* everything went well at the party. (happy)
2 He goes rock climbing on the weekend. (usual)
3 It was hot on the bus. (uncomfortable)
4 There was a snowstorm, so we couldn't go climbing. (unfortunate)
5 I am asked why I love taking risks. (frequent)
6 She speaks French. (good)
7 The hotel was cheap. (reasonable)
8 I studied the route before I set off. (careful)
9 Thrill seekers find activities like white-water rafting exciting. (extreme)
10 I don't like taking risks. (person)

**b** Complete the chart with the adverbs in **5a**.

| Adverb of manner | Adverb of frequency | Adverb to modify an adjective | Sentence adverb |
|---|---|---|---|
| | | | *happily* |

**6** Put the words in the correct order to make sentences.

1 skillfully climbed she mountain the
2 hardly risks takes he ever
3 discuss carefully this to need you
4 in their danger want lives people often some
5 the seasick surprisingly voyage nobody on got
6 is highly he sailor experienced a

**7** Correct the sentences. Mark (✓) three correct sentences.

1 Extreme sports are gradually becoming more expensive.
2 We take usually all the necessary precautions.
3 She's a thrill seeker, so always she's trying new activities.
4 My sailing teacher talks very fast!
5 Diving with sharks is dangerous extremely.
6 Interestingly, the first bungee jump took place on Vanuatu, a Pacific island.
7 I go sometimes rock climbing on my vacations.
8 My boyfriend can read very well maps.

## BRING IT TOGETHER

**8** Choose the correct options to complete the text.

### This Year's Weirdest Weather

Onlookers were astonished to see lightning during the eruption of Mount Shinmoedake in January. While people (1)*had watched / were watching* the eruption of the Japanese volcano, strange lights appeared in the sky above it. Local people (2)*had never seen / never had seen* anything like it before, which was not surprising as experts (3)*are still not / are not still* exactly certain why it occurred.

Planes were left waiting at Lagos airport in October as a mysterious fog appeared in Nigeria. The fog covered everything with white dust, so many people (4)*had walked / were walking* around with gray hair and clothes. By the time it finally ended, some towns (5)*hadn't seen / weren't seeing* the sun for four days. Afterward, local experts explained that the dust (6)*had blown / was blowing* into the country from the Sahara to create the strange effect.

At the end of the year, a sudden storm hit Perth, Australia. Three centimeters of rain fell in just fifteen minutes, and several buildings collapsed after the rain (7)*had damaged / was damaging* their roofs. While the floodwaters (8)*had risen / were rising*, many people decided to leave their houses. Most people (9)*left calmly their homes / left their homes calmly* without any signs of panic, once again showing how (10)*resilient amazingly / amazingly resilient* the Australian people are in the face of disaster.

## FUNCTIONAL LANGUAGE
### Giving warnings

**1** Complete the words.

Hi Mick

I can't believe that you're going on safari! In your e-mail, you asked me for some advice. Here it is!

(1)R__________ to get full medical insurance because you'll come into contact with wild animals. It's also important to see the doctor to be vaccinated before you leave. You definitely (2)s__________ forget to take antimalarial tablets, either. Malaria's a real problem in some areas, so you want to be (3)c__________ if you're going to be in any of them. You (4)m__________ want to take a mosquito net, too, to give you extra protection.

Make (5)s__________ you take an adapter to recharge your camera or your cell phone. Speaking of photography, you should buy extra memory cards because you'll take so many pictures. You (6)m__________ also want to pack sunscreen. I (7)w__________ buy that kind of thing while you're overseas because it's cheaper at home. You could also buy a guide to the birds of Africa because you'll see lots, and it's impossible to remember their names.

Otherwise, you (8)d__________ want to worry too much. It's going to be a lot of fun!

Bye for now

Joseph

## LISTENING
### Listening for specific information

**1** **a** 3.2 You are going to listen to the weather forecast for South Africa. Listen and number the places in the order you hear them.

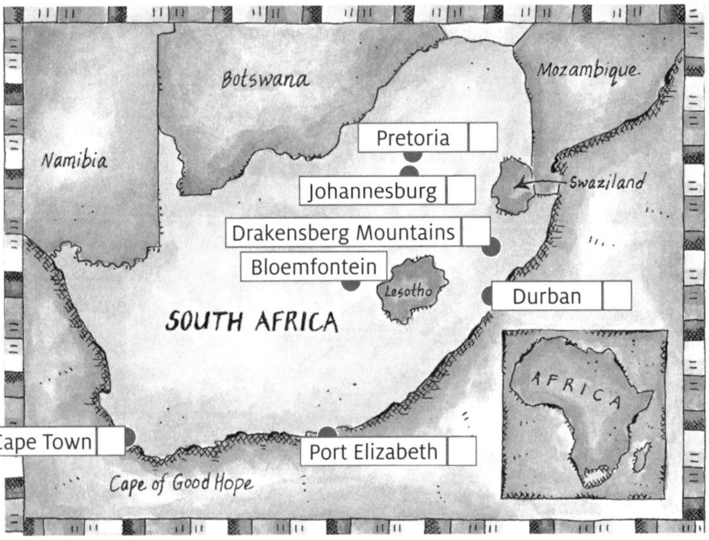


**b** How many severe weather warnings did you hear? Where were they for? __________

**2** **a** Read the weather forecast summary. In which blank(s) is/are the missing word(s)

a a number? __________
b a noun? __________
c an adjective? __________
d an adverb? __________

| | |
|---|---|
| **Cape Town** | (1)__________ in the early morning—remember to drive (2)__________! |
| **Durban** | clear (3)__________ and (4)__________ weather throughout the day. |
| **Pretoria** | maximum temperature of (5)__________ °C. There is a possibility of (6)__________ midafternoon. |
| **Drakensberg Mountains** | risk of (7)__________ and large (8)__________ in some areas. |

**b** Listen again. Complete the summary with one word in each blank.

**STRATEGY** Before you listen, read the questions carefully and decide what kind of information you need to listen for. Remember, you don't need to understand every word you hear!

## READING Referencing devices

**1** **a** Read the text. Match sentences a–g to blanks 1–6. There is one sentence that you do not need.

a The next step is the hardest and will test how resilient the six men really are.
b There were more than 100 experiments programmed.
c One from Colombia, France and China with the others all from Russia.
d They hadn't even left the Earth's atmosphere.
e Their only contact with the outside world was via the Internet.
f For example, what is the effect of radiation on travelers in deep space?
g Then they dug a hole in the planet surface to take rock and dust samples.

**b** Read the text again. Then look at the Strategy box. Underline examples of the three patterns in the text

**2** Answer the questions.

1 What did the men take to place on the surface of Mars?
______
2 How long was the mission?
______
3 Why was communication not instant?
______
4 What other name is given for Mars in the text?
______
5 What institution helped the men prepare?
______
6 How did the astronauts practice their medical skills?
______

**STRATEGY** To help you understand a long text, look out for patterns that show you how ideas connect together. These might be

- a series of phrases (e.g., *first, then, next*)
- linking phrases that connect one idea to another (e.g., *however, actually, for example*)
- or words that replace an earlier idea in the text (e.g., *this, that, these*).

# Mission to Mars

On Monday, February 14, 2011, human beings finally walked across the surface of Mars. First, they investigated the local terrain. (1) ______ After leaving three flags representing the international crew—from China, Russia and Europe—the courageous explorers returned to the safety of the their spacecraft, Mars500... except that it didn't happen quite like that.

In fact, the three men were walking along the floor of a building in Russia. They hadn't traveled through space. (2) ______ They were taking part in the Mars500 project, a simulation to see how human beings react on a long journey through space.

We are not at the stage of a manned mission to Mars yet because there are still a lot of unanswered questions. (3) ______ We don't know yet. Before they can take the risk of sending a spacecraft across the solar system, scientists also need to know how six people react to living in such a small area for over a year and a half.

To do this, they developed the Mars500 project, where six volunteers agreed to spend 519 days in a spaceship, separated from the outside world—and pretending to go through space. (4) ______ However, even that had a 20-minute delay to represent the time it takes messages to travel across space from Earth.

Before their arrival on the red planet, the men had been performing a series of tasks to see how resourceful they needed to be. (5) ______ These included performing mock operations as there would be no access to surgeons or other experts during the trip. Thankfully, they were well-prepared because they had spent

months practicing with the staff of Mainz University before the trip began, and they performed their operation (on a model—not a real person!) without any major errors.

(6) ______ They must turn around and return to Earth, facing another difficult 240 days on board. Then finally they can meet their waiting families and tell them their stories of the year and a half that they spent traveling... nowhere.

# PROGRESS TEST 1

## GRAMMAR & VOCABULARY (25 points)

**1** Rewrite the sentences using the word in bold. Do not change the word given. (*10 points*)

0 Kostas is your manager—is that correct?
*Kostas is your manager, isn't he?* **isn't**

1 Who was this blog written by?
__________ **wrote**

2 The optician tested my eyes.
__________ **had**

3 It's not normal for me to get up at 6 a.m.
__________ **used**

4 I started working here five years ago.
__________ **have**

5 I was waiting for an hour before the bus arrived.
__________ **been**

**2** Complete the sentences with the words from the box. (*8 points*)

| acupuncturist antibiotics binoculars bruise fog gale ~~partner~~ passenger raft |
|---|

0 Rachel and I started a business together—she's my *partner* .
1 I want to see what's on the mountaintop. Pass me the _____ .
2 Tomas has a bad _____ on his arm—it's turned purple!
3 It was difficult to drive because of the thick _____ .
4 Several trees were blown down during the _____ .
5 There was no one on the train but me. I was the only _____ .
6 After she visited the _____ , my grandmother's back pain disappeared.
7 We have a life _____ in case there's an accident on board the ship.
8 Luckily, we can treat a bacterial infection with _____ .

**3** Match 1–7 to a–h. (*7 points*)

0 Bad news. Sharon and her boyfriend have broken *d* .
1 Frank and Hans are good friends. They really get _____ .
2 If you want Mary to be your girlfriend, you have to ask her _____ .
3 The nurse asked to take my _____ .
4 The surgeon can't see you because she's performing a(n) _____ in the operating room.
5 A lifeguard had to rescue me at the beach after I got into _____ .
6 I have some bad news for you. Something has gone terribly _____ .
7 You can only buy this medicine if the doctor writes you a _____ .

a out   b operation   c wrong   ~~d up~~
e trouble   f prescription   g along   h temperature

## READING (25 points)

**1** Choose the best title for the text. (*3 points*)

1 The Death of the Guidebook
2 Guidebooks Go Online
3 Why I Still Use Guidebooks

**2** Complete blanks 1–6 in the text with missing sentences a–g. (*12 points*)

a Furthermore, reviewers usually say something about themselves.
b With a few quick tweets, you can find the latest restaurants, hotels and places to see.
c It's voice-activated.
d He was a complete snob!
e Well... no, not anymore.
f That person might give a place a good review just because the owners were nice to him/her.
g Plane tickets? Passport? Travel insurance?

Sunscreen? Check! Cell phone? Check! (0) *g* Check! Check! Check! Guidebook? (1) _____ People just don't want them these days. Like many other reference works like dictionaries, encyclopedias and atlases, the day of the guidebook might be over. It's all the fault of the World Wide Web.

While carrying our tablets and laptops, we can get much more information faster over the Internet. Twitter is one of the best means of getting top tips for your next travel location. (2) _____ People will also tell you the places that are closest to you.

If it's reviews you're after, what guidebook could match websites like Trip Advisor? In your guidebook, you get just one person's opinion of a hotel. (3) _____ And of course, as soon as a place is mentioned in a famous guidebook, room prices go up overnight. That cheap stay has just become one of the most expensive beds in the city!

Even the people selling the trips are getting involved. On Booking.com you can read reviews from a range of users. (4) _____ This is a real advantage because we all have different needs when we travel. With peer reviews, you can see whether a hotel is good for people like you. When you read a guidebook, on the other hand, you hope that the author thinks like you, but that's not always the case. I once went on a trip to Brazil with a guidebook, and I really disagreed with the author. (5) _____ If a beach wasn't totally isolated, kilometers and kilometers from the nearest house, he hated it! Personally, I prefer to sunbathe on a beach near my hotel.

The truly amazing thing is that the Internet is changing incredibly quickly. In the USA, they've just started using an iPhone app called Siri. (6) _____ You talk into it, and it processes all the information on the web to get the best travel information. However, it only works in the States at the moment.

So, good-bye guidebook authors—we're all experts now!

**3** Answer the questions. (*10 points*)

1 What other books does the author mention in the article, apart from guidebooks?

______________________

2 Which website is useful if you don't want to walk a long way from your present location? Why?

______________________

3 What happens when a hotel appears in a guidebook?

______________________

4 Why did the author of the article disagree with a guidebook author?

______________________

5 Why is Siri not yet good for someone traveling around the world?

______________________

## LISTENING (*25 points*)

**1** T1 Listen to five short conversations. Where are the people? (*5 points*)

Conversation 1 ______________
Conversation 2 ______________
Conversation 3 ______________
Conversation 4 ______________
Conversation 5 ______________

**2** Listen again. Match the speakers to the relationships. There is one answer that you don't need. (*10 points*)

In which conversation (1–5), are the speakers

a in-laws? ____
b a stranger and a passerby? ____
c acquaintances? ____
d teammates? ____
e colleagues? ____
f husband and wife? ____

**3** Choose the correct options. (*10 points*)

1 In conversation 1, what does Barry want for his sailing trip?
  a Some clothing.
  b Some medical equipment.
  c Some technology.
2 In conversation 2, What is Janet's job?
  a A homeopath. b A midwife. c A pharmacist.
3 In conversation 3, why is Lee not feeling well?
  a Because of something he ate.
  b Because of the hot weather.
  c Because of an injection.
4 In conversation 4, what is the family going to do?
  a Go on some rides.
  b Visit the zoo.
  c Walk around a museum.
5 In conversation 5, why were Harry and Pamela successful?
  a They're really determined.
  b They're really experienced.
  c They're really reckless.

## WRITING (*25 points*)

**1** Complete the blog post with one word in each blank. Do you agree with the advice? (*5 points*)

Help! I'm 16, and I really want to go on an ice-climbing trip with my friends. The problem is that my parents think it's too dangerous, and they don't want me to go. What should I do?

Jess

Hi Jess
This is a difficult one. The first thing (0) *is* to ensure that your ice-climbing trip is being organized by professionals. You (1) ______ overestimate how important this is. The mountains are dangerous, and you need to know your instructor is qualified to deal with emergencies. Whatever you (2) ______, don't go with an unqualified group leader.
After you have checked this, my advice (3) ______ be to do lots of research on ice-climbing that you can give to your parents. It's important (4) ______ show them that ice-climbing is pretty safe if you do it the right way. If I (5) ______ you, I'd also contact the organizers of the ice-climbing trip and ask them to talk to your family. That way, your parents will feel better about the trip, and perhaps they'll change their minds.
Good luck!

Xenia

**2** Read the blog post. Write a reply to Felipe, giving him some advice. (*20 points*)

Hi everyone,
My son's 18, and he's just heard that he has to check into the hospital for an operation on his leg. It's really bad news because he wanted to start college next month, but now he has to wait until next year. He's feeling really depressed and frustrated because all his friends are going away to study, but he has to spend two months in a hospital ward. What can I do to make him feel better? Do you have any ideas? He loves learning languages and traveling.
Thanks,
Felipe

# 4 REINVENTION

## VOCABULARY

### Appearance

**1** **a** Read the clues. Complete the crossword with words that describe appearance.

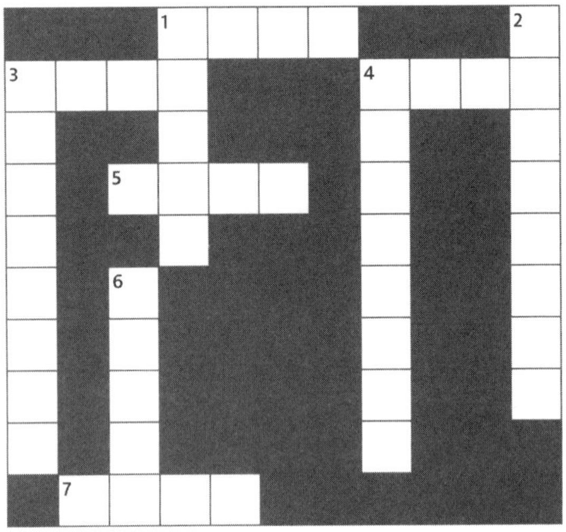


**Across**

1 This means "without hair on your head."
3 You have this kind of complexion if you are not feeling well.
4 This describes light-colored skin or hair.
5 The color an elderly person's hair turns.
7 When you change your hair color using chemicals, you have hair like this.

**Down**

1 Men can grow this hair on their chin.
2 Lines you get on your skin as you get older.
3 If you wear jewelry in your ears or nose, you probably have one of these.
4 These are small brown marks that some people get on their skin.
6 Your hair is like this if it is not straight.

**b** Circle the word that doesn't work in each sentence.

1 I have *beards / freckles / wrinkles* around my nose.
2 My skin is naturally very *dyed / fair / dark*.
3 My sister doesn't have straight hair—it's *curly / pale / wavy*.
4 Would you ever get a *tattoo / piercing / complexion*?
5 Lots of men have a *bald / beard / mustache*.

**2** Choose the correct options to complete the sentences.

1 My uncle's *growing / making* a mustache, and it's already very long.
2 We're going to the bathroom to *get / put* on our makeup.
3 My hair's getting really long, so I need to *do / get* a haircut.
4 Dirk looks great bald—that's why he always *cuts / shaves* his head.
5 I was going to *get / make* a piercing in my nose, but then I changed my mind.
6 If you want to *change / grow* your look, let's go shopping and get completely new clothes.

### Describing people

**3** Write the letters in parentheses in the correct order to complete the words.

Hi Sharon

Sorry I haven't written for a while, but I've been really busy! Moving to the ballet school in Russia has been a complete life change. The teachers here are really strict. They're not at all as (1)__________ __________ (*dlia-cabk*) as the ones back home in Brasilia! It's also difficult because my Russian is really bad, and I never say anything. That's unusual for me because I'm really (2)__________ (*latkitaev*) and (3)__________ (*ogutingo*), as you know! The worst thing is that because I was worried about the language, I was very (4)__________-__________ (*flse osciouncus*) about my dancing at first, too.

Luckily, I'm sharing a room with Vladimir, and he's great. He speaks perfect English, and he's really (5)__________ (*iyttw*). He introduced me to all his friends, who are all very (6)__________ (*villey*) and invite me to lots of parties! But don't worry—I haven't forgotten my studies. Vlad is really (7)__________ (*addecited*) like me, so we spend a lot of time practicing.

In fact, because of his help, I've become a lot more (8)__________ (*ofncitend*), which is good because we have a big show next week!

Talk soon!

Roberto

P.S. Picture attached!

## Vocabulary Extension
### Work

**4** **a** Read the text. Match the words in bold to definitions a–f.

### Changing Direction

This time last year, I was working at a big bank. Everything seemed perfect—I had just received a **promotion** and a raise. Then my employers had to **fire** a lot of people. I lost my job and my high **salary**, and I didn't know what to do.

After a month of unsuccessful job applications, I started to work as a **freelance** writer. I asked my old boss for a **reference**, and he wrote a lot of positive things about me. Now I write blogs and articles about financial issues, and I've decided to **train** to be a journalist. Losing my job forced me to change my career, and I actually feel a lot happier now.

a to lay off from a job, to let go. ________
b when you are given a better, more important job. ________
c to learn the skills needed for a particular job. ________
d a regular, fixed payment given to an employee. ________
e a statement describing a person's skills and work experience, written by a colleague. ________
f earning money by working for several different companies. ________

**b** Complete the chart with the words in bold in **5a**.

| Nouns | Adjectives | Verbs |
| --- | --- | --- |
| | | |

## Bring It Together

**5** Complete the conversation with the words from the box. There is one word that you don't need.

dark dedicated fire laid-back lively look promotion salary shave talkative

**A** Hi, Tina!

**B** Hi Tom! Wow, I love your profile photo! You've completely changed your (1)________ since we were in school. Your clothes, hair, everything!

**A** It's true.

**B** Isn't your hair naturally (2)________ ?

**A** Yeah, it's bleached blonde now. Do you like it? I was going to (3)________ my head this week, but I decided to change my hairstyle like this instead.

**B** Well, it suits you. So you're living the surfer lifestyle now?

**A** Yeah. It's a very nice, (4)________ life, very relaxing.

**B** You're so lucky! I'm working in a bank, and it's really stressful. I just got a (5)________, so my job is more important now, but I'm busy all the time. And no one talks at work. I hate that because I'm really (6)________ .

**A** But it's a good job, isn't it? I'm just giving surfing lessons. My (7)________ isn't great, so I have to live with my parents.

**B** Are you studying as well?

**A** Yeah, I am. I'm studying drama. I've been really (8)________ this year. I've been working very hard! The lessons are really (9)________ and energetic, so it's fun.

**B** I studied business administration—and that wasn't fun at all!

## GRAMMAR
### Present perfect or past simple?

**1** Choose the correct options to complete the text.

(1)*You probably heard / You've probably heard* stories about how future stars were discovered on the street, but Alexander Beck's story is especially amazing. Earlier this year, the teenager (2)*ran into / has run into* fashion scout Cesar Perin in a Cambridge bookstore. Perin (3)*immediately noticed / has immediately noticed* Alexander's unusual look. From that moment, Alexander (4)*worked / has worked* with Perin as the latest top male model. He (5)*already appeared / has already appeared* in *Vogue* magazine and has more big projects to come. His life (6)*changed / has changed* completely from the time when he was a normal schoolboy. In fact, before his modeling career, Alexander (7)*worked / has worked* in his local fish and chip restaurant! Since quitting that job, his income (8)*rose / has risen* enormously as he now walks down the catwalk for Prada in fashion shows across Europe. At a time when it (9)*became / has become* almost impossible to turn on the TV without seeing competitions for the next top model, Alex's story is incredibly surprising. He (10)*didn't fight / hasn't fought* to appear on TV like thousands of other hopefuls—in fact, he had never considered modeling before that trip to the bookstore a few months ago.

**2** Complete the sentences with *already* or *yet*.

1 Cora's on a diet. She's ____________ lost a lot of weight.
2 Dean wants to get another tattoo. I think he's crazy—he has eight ____________ !
3 Has Jim started his new job ____________ ?
4 Julia's only twenty-one, but she's ____________ started using anti-aging cream.
5 I really need a haircut, but I haven't been to the beauty salon ____________ .
6 Jane hasn't opened her new salon ____________ , but I think it's going to be a great success!

**3** **a** Complete the pairs of sentences using the words in parentheses. In each pair, use one verb in the past simple and one verb in the present perfect.

1 i The new tanning salon on Main Street ____________ (open) last week. *b*
  ii The new tanning salon on Main Street ____________ (not/open/yet). ______
2 i Olle ____________ (shave) his head yesterday because he wanted to change his look. ______
  ii Olle ____________ (never/shave) his head before, but now he wants a new look. ______
3 i I've started going to the gym, but I ____________ (not/build up) my muscles yet. ______
  ii I've started going to the gym. I ____________ (go) three times on the weekend! ______
4 i Julio's only twenty-nine, but his hair ____________ (already/start) to turn gray. ______
  ii Julio's only twenty-nine, but his hair ____________ (turn) gray when he was very young. ______

**b** Match pictures a–h to the sentences in **3a**.

a

b

c

d

e

f

g

h

## Present perfect simple or continuous?

**4** Complete the sentences with the correct form of the words in parentheses: present perfect or present perfect continuous.

1 Maria's obsessed with having a tan. She ____________ (go) to the tanning salon three times already this week.
2 Gabrielle ____________ (write) her autobiography; it's almost finished.
3 I ____________ (have) four piercings since I was 18. I really regret getting them.
4 He ____________ (grow) a beard for two weeks; it's getting very thick.
5 Since she got out of prison, she ____________ (try) to rebuild her image.
6 He ____________ (direct) 15 movies and is now working on his sixteenth.
7 She ____________ (look) for a job for two months. I hope she'll get an interview soon.
8 Janine ____________ (dye) her hair red, blue and green, but now it's her natural color again.

**5** Which sentences are correct? Mark (✓) the correct box: a, b or both a and b.

1 a I've had my hair cut today.
  b I've been having a haircut today.
  a ☐ b ☐ both a and b ☐
2 a Wow! George has really changed his look!
  b Wow! George has really been changing his look!
  a ☐ b ☐ both a and b ☐
3 a He's written about his experiences as a tattoo artist.
  b He's been writing about his experiences as a tattoo artist.
  a ☐ b ☐ both a and b ☐
4 a José looks different because he's shaved his head.
  b José looks different because he's been shaving his head.
  a ☐ b ☐ both a and b ☐
5 a I'm looking for a job, so I've sent ten e-mails this week.
  b I'm looking for a job, so I've been sending ten e-mails this week.
  a ☐ b ☐ both a and b ☐
6 a The new campaign has gained support over the last few weeks.
  b The new campaign has been gaining support over the last few weeks.
  a ☐ b ☐ both a and b ☐

## Uses of the *-ing* form

**6** Change one word in each sentence to the *-ing* form.

1 *No smoke in school.* *smoking*
2 The band's new song is all about reinvent yourself.
3 Use a tanning bed to get a tan is very popular in many countries.
4 I can't get used to see her with purple hair!
5 Angela is much better at English than me—her speak skills are really good.
6 If you want to improve your Spanish, have you considered take a trip to Mexico?
7 I always enjoy watch French movies on TV, although I can't always understand everything.
8 I'm looking forward to go to America so I can practice my English.

## Bring It Together

**7** Choose the correct options to complete the text.

### Crisis in the Carteret Islands

As climate change continues, the people of the Carteret Islands [1]*had / have had* to accept that their lives are going to change completely. For centuries, the women of the islands [2]*have owned / have been owning* the land, so today one woman, local leader Ursula Rakova, is working with her people to help them with this change. Due to rising sea levels, her own island of Huene [3]*has disappeared / has been disappearing* beneath the ocean. She can see the damage increasing all the time.

There are approximately 3,000 islanders, and [4]*moving / having moved* them all is an enormous task. Day by day, people [5]*have been going / went* to Bougainville on the mainland to start a new life. However, [6]*leaving / leave* their homes is difficult, and many people feel desperate.

Since the sea levels began to rise, Ms. Rakova [7]*has been fighting / fought* to build new houses and schools for her people. After [8]*waited / waiting* a long time for government help, she finally decided to lead the relocation program herself. She [9]*formed / has formed* her own charity in 2006 to tell the world about her people's crisis. Her message is clear. Although climate change [10]*didn't affect / hasn't affected* every country yet, it is already destroying lives in many of the poorest parts of the globe.

## FUNCTIONAL LANGUAGE Complaining

**1** Put the words in parentheses in the correct order to complete the conversations.

1 At home

A Oh no! They're playing music again.

B I know. (1) ___________ (it's nerves really my on getting).

A And (2) ___________ (playing that they're always song)! Don't they have any other CDs?

B They were playing music at three o'clock this morning.

A (3) ___________ (me crazy driving it's). I'm going to go over and complain.

2 At work

C I'm having real problems with my new clients. My contact person, Amy, calls me all the time—at night on the weekend...

D That is a little unreasonable. I will talk to her about it.

C Also, (4) ___________ (way really it the me annoys) she tells me to do things. It's like she's my manager—not you.

D It sounds difficult, but they're important clients.

C I know, but (5) ___________ (you never they thank say) for anything. They're really rude!

3 In a band

E I'm so tired of the band.

F Is it because of Mike?

E Yeah, it is. He's a great singer, but (6) ___________ (the can't I way he stand) keeps giving everyone orders.

F I know. (7) ___________ (exactly on people strong skills not he's). He thinks he's the boss.

E And I started the band! It's my group—not his!

F (8) ___________ (most the that thing me annoys) is that he never asks us about the songs. He just chooses them and we play them!

E Well I think we should leave the band and start a new one of our own!

## LISTENING Prediction

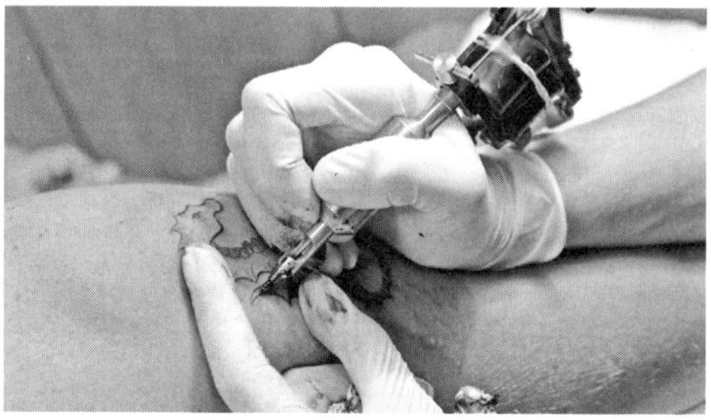

**1** **a** You are going to listen to an interview with a tattoo artist from Macao. Look at the questions. What do you think the answers will be?

1 Why did you become a tattoo artist?

___________

2 What kind of character do you need to be a tattoo artist?

___________

3 What kind of people had tattoos in the past?

___________

4 When do you refuse to tattoo someone?

___________

5 What kind of images are popular as tattoos?

___________

6 How do you feel about your job?

___________

**b** 4.1 Listen and check your answers. How many of your predictions were correct?

**2** **a** Complete the sentences.

1 My father and my grandfather were both tattoo artists, so it's kind of a ___________ business.
2 Even today, if you go on a job ___________ or something, you might need to cover up your tattoo.
3 Just this ___________ I spoke to a guy about his tattoo design, and he changed his mind twice while he was talking to me.
4 A tattoo of a rabbit represents ___________ , for example.
5 A tattoo of a ___________ represents a fun or a lively person.
6 I enjoy helping people change their ___________ .
7 I see myself as part of a tradition going back ___________ of years.

**b** Listen again and check your answers.

**STRATEGY** Before listening to an audio, try to guess what the speaker will say. If you know the person's nationality, age, gender, profession, etc., it can help you guess their opinions. Don't forget to look at any pictures for clues about the speaker.

## WRITING Informal writing

**1** Read the e-mail quickly and answer the questions.

1 What job does Jay have? ______________________

2 Who helped her find the job? ______________________

3 How long did she have to wait for the result of her interview? ______________________

Hey everyone,

How's it going? You won't believe what I'm about to tell you. You know that I came home to Singapore last year after we were all studying in Los Angeles? Well, I've been looking for work for ages, but I've finally found a job... I'm going to work for the police as an interpreter!

It's kind of weird—doing police work is a big change from reading literature and writing essays! My dad saw the want ad for a job in the paper, and he told me to get in touch with them. At first I wasn't sure, but I did go for an interview... and they gave me the job then and there! It does help that I speak English, German, Chinese, Malay and "Singlish" (our version of English—remember?). And using my languages is what I most enjoy, so I guess the work will be interesting.

Anyway, the interview was crazy. I really dressed up—I took out all my piercings, washed the red dye out of my hair and put on this very uncool jacket. It was like my school uniform or something! My sister was so shocked by my "transformation" that she took my picture (attached)!

Anyway, they must have liked it because I start work on Monday. I think I'll only do it for a year or so and then find something different. But a job's a job, right?!

Anyway, miss you!

Love,

Jay

**2** Read the e-mail again. Find informal equivalents for the formal words and phrases.

| Formal | Informal |
|---|---|
| (1) Dear all | *Hey everyone* |
| (2) How are you? | |
| (3) a long time | |
| (4) slightly | |
| (5) to contact | |
| (6) immediately | |
| (7) unfashionable | |
| (8) I assume | |
| (9) around 12 months | |
| (10) Best wishes | |

**3** Write a reply to Jay. Respond to her news and tell her about what you have been doing recently. Use ideas from the Strategy box to help you.

**STRATEGY** When you write an informal e-mail, you can...
- use informal words and expressions (*Hey, kind of, I think*, etc.)
- use contractions (*I'm, I've, it's*, etc.)
- use less formal punctuation like dashes (–) and exclamation marks (!)
- use short or incomplete sentences and questions (*remember?, miss you!*).

# 5 FOOD FOR THOUGHT

## VOCABULARY
### Food

**1** Put the letters in parentheses in the correct order to make cooking words.

**My Idea of Comfort Food – Margaret Foo**

When I go home to Malaysia, there's one food that I always want: *nasi lemak*. It's our national dish, and my mother makes the best! It's rice that is (1) ____________ (smeedat) with coconut milk and eaten with various ingredients like raw cucumber, spices and a (2) ____________ (delibo) egg, as well as (3) ____________ (tedroas) peanuts. It's really adaptable so many people eat it with other Malaysian dishes, like *rendang*. That's beef that is cooked for several hours to absorb special spices. I've even seen *nasi lemak* served in coastal towns as an accompaniment to seafood (4) ____________ (legirdl) over a charcoal fire.

However, *nasi lemak* is most often eaten for breakfast—street vendors like the lady in the photo often sell it served in a banana leaf. If I can't get *nasi lemak*, I usually choose *roti canai*. It's a kind of bread, but it's not (5) ____________ (kadeb) in an oven like Western bread. Instead it's (6) ____________ (refid) in hot oil—it's delicious when served with condensed milk. Yum yum yum!

**2** Circle the word that <u>doesn't</u> work in each sentence.

1. This chili sauce is delicious; it's so *mild / spicy / sweet*.
2. This dessert isn't very good for your health because it's very *creamy / crispy / greasy*.
3. I love this tropical lemon drink. It's very *chewy / sweet / sour*, but really refreshing.
4. This soup isn't very tasty. In fact, it's really *bland / mild / salty*.
5. When lettuce is fresh, it's perfect for a salad—really *bitter / crispy / crunchy*.

**3** **a** Complete the words in the shopping lists for dishes 1–3.

**1**

tomatoes
(1) b _ _ _ l
(2) o _ _ _ _ o _ _
(3) g _ _ _ _ c
spaghetti
(4) b _ _ _ _
p _ _ _ _ r

**2**

apples
butter
flour
sugar
(5) c _ _ n _ _ _ n
(6) v _ _ _ _ _ a

**3**

chicken
(7) c _ _ _ i
(8) s _ _ s _ _ _ _
(9) w _ _ _
v _ _ _ _ _ r
green pepper
(10) c _ r _ _ _ _ _ r

**b** Do you ever cook dishes like these?

## Business

**4** Match 1–6 to a–f.

1 Our customers always buy our jeans and no other company's
2 Most banks today have to be multinationals
3 You'll find drugstores run by this company in every town in the country
4 My restaurant has another company's name
5 Our main target market is children aged 3–5
6 All the local bookstores are closing

a because they can't compete with big Internet stores.
b because it's part of a franchise.
c because they're all part of a chain.
d because they love toys like this.
e because they inspire real brand loyalty.
f because they work in markets all over the world.

## Vocabulary Extension

### Cooking equipment

**5** **a** Read the descriptions. Match items in the picture a–h to the words in bold in sentences 1–8.

1 A **wok** is used in Chinese cuisine to fry food at hot temperatures. ____
2 **Cutlery** is a group word for knives, forks and spoons. ____
3 A **saucepan** is used to boil food on the stove. ____
4 **Chopsticks** are two pieces of wood that people use for eating in many parts of the world. ____
5 Cut vegetables on a **cutting board** so the knife doesn't damage the countertop. ____
6 To make this soup, you purée the cooked vegetables in a **blender**. ____
7 After you've cooked it, put the pasta in a **sieve** to drain off the water. ____
8 Use a **frying pan** to make fried eggs or an omelet. ____

**b** 5.1 Listen and check.

## Bring It Together

**6** Complete the blog post with words from the box. There is one word that you don't need.

| bitter | bland | blender | brand loyalty |
|---|---|---|---|
| compete | creamy | multinationals | |
| sieve | target market | vanilla | vinegar |

Drinks | Restaurants | Contacts | Comments (2)

### Soft Drinks around the World

With globalization, the big (1)__________ like Coca-Cola and Pepsi seem to dominate the soft drink industry. However, look a little further and you find many local soft drink companies that are able to (2)__________ with the big two. Here we profile some.

Asia is a key (3)__________ for many soft drink manufacturers. Korea's Milkis is popular both at home and abroad. It's made with milk, giving it a (4)__________ taste. In some parts of Mexico, many prefer Tonicol, a refreshing drink that is flavored with (5)__________ .

If you don't like sweet drinks, Italy has a range of (6)__________ ones, including Chinotto and Beverly (which tastes like tonic water). Finally, visitors to Brazil will be familiar with Guaraná. It's a fruity drink that enjoys huge (7)__________ throughout the country; its sales there may be higher than those of Coca-Cola! So next time you're in a new place, why not try something different?

Alternatively, it's easy to make your own soft drinks—just purée some fruit in an electric (8)__________ . Put it through a (9)__________ to remove the seeds, add mineral water and in seconds you'll have your own soft drink! Homemade drinks always taste great; they're flavorful and never (10)__________ !

Done

# GRAMMAR

## Future forms

**1** Which sentences are correct? Mark (✓) the correct box: a, b or both a and b.

1 a I'm going to have dinner with my brother after work today.
b I'm having dinner with my brother after work today.
a ☐ b ☐ both a and b ☐

2 a There are fewer cacao farmers every year, so I think the price of chocolate will continue to rise.
b There are fewer cacao farmers every year, so I think the price of chocolate is continuing to rise.
a ☐ b ☐ both a and b ☐

3 a The sales meeting starts in five minutes.
b The sales meeting's going to start in five minutes.
a ☐ b ☐ both a and b ☐

4 a The new franchise open next month. We need another meeting to finalize plans.
b The new franchise is opening next month. We need another meeting to finalize plans.
a ☐ b ☐ both a and b ☐

5 a That meal was delicious, Olle. I cook for you next week, I promise!
b That meal was delicious, Olle. I'll cook for you next week, I promise!
a ☐ b ☐ both a and b ☐

**2** Replace the underlined verbs with either *will* or the present continuous for the future. (All these sentences are already correct.) Write your answers below.

M Wow, Phueng, look at all these ingredients on your shopping list: chili, garlic, coconut paste! What (1)are you going to cook with all of them? You obviously have some interesting plans.

P (2)I'm going to prepare a green curry. It's a specialty of Thailand. (3)Som and I are going to make it for the end of semester party.

M (4)Isn't the chili going to make it a little hot?

P Don't worry, Miranda. My curry (5)isn't going to be very spicy. (6)It's going to taste nice and mild.

M Great. Well, I think (7)the other students are going to love it.

P So that's my plan. What's yours?

M I don't have one. (8)I'm not going to come to the party.

P Really? Why not?

M (9)I'm going to see my sister tomorrow evening. She just had her baby!

P Wow, that's great news!

M I'm sorry I won't be able to try the curry—I'm sure everyone will love it.

P Don't worry. I don't think (10)we're going to eat all of it, so I can save some for you to eat afterward.

M Great! Thanks, Phueng!

1 ______ 6 ______
2 ______ 7 ______
3 ______ 8 ______
4 ______ 9 ______
5 ______ 10 ______

## Clauses

**3** Choose the correct options to complete the sentences.

1 I'll go straight to the restaurant *as soon as / until* I've finished work.
2 You can't look at your cell phone *before / once* the meeting begins.
3 We can't cook dinner *once / unless* we go to the supermarket!
4 Prices will continue to rise *after / until* food production costs go down.
5 Finish your main course *before / as soon as* you eat dessert, OK?
6 My ride to work takes two hours, so I usually have coffee *after / until* I arrive.

**4** Complete the sentences with the correct form of the words in parentheses.

1 Don't buy food there unless you ______ it's fresh. (know)
2 As soon as the meeting ______ , call me. (finish)
3 Once Nadine ______ the USA, she can write her report about American food production. (visit)
4 I can't cook dinner until I ______ some meat and vegetables. (buy)
5 They won't open a franchise there unless the market ______ in the next few months. (change)
6 Dave will call you once he ______ a table in the restaurant. (have)
7 Let's have a cup of coffee before we ______ . (leave)
8 Ask Iris to call me after she ______ to the doctor. (speak)

## Future continuous & future perfect

**5** **a** Put the words in the correct order to make sentences.

1 be / people / tonight / will / making / 20 / Rita / for / dinner

______________________

2 started / 3 p.m. / Rita / cooking / will / by / have

______________________

3 have / arrived / seven / the / will / by / guests

______________________

4 by / eaten / everyone / will / a / eleven / lot / have

______________________

5 at / this / will / time / Rita / be / relaxing / tomorrow

______________________

**b** Which sentences in **5a** are

a future continuous? _____ b future perfect? _____

**6** Choose the correct options to complete the blog post.

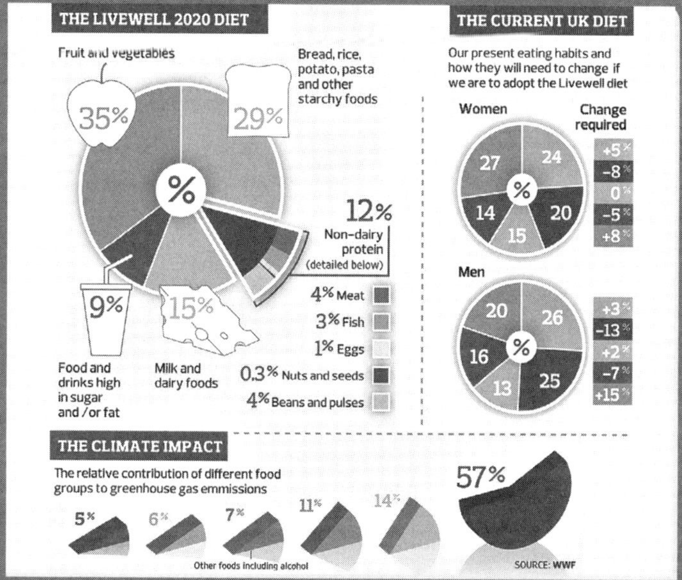


### LIVE AND LET LIVE

By 2050, the world's population (1)*will be rising / will have risen* to nine billion people. If that's true, by the middle of the century, large amounts of jungle (2)*will already be turning into / will already have turned into* giant farms for meat and dairy production. After the disappearance of their forest homes, a large number of animal species (3)*will be becoming / will have become* extinct, too.

How can we prevent that terrible future? One way is the WWF's Livewell diet. They hope more people (4)*will be following / will have followed* it over the next few years. My family (5)*will be trying / will have tried* this out for the next twelve months. On December 31, (6)*we'll be finding out / we'll have found out* how easy it was to follow.

The idea is simple. If we reduce the amount of meat and dairy we eat, we can reduce the impact of farming on the environment. The WWF hopes the expansion of the world's farmland (7)*will be stopping / will have stopped* completely by the end of 2050—and our grandchildren (8)*will still be enjoying / will still have enjoyed* the natural world.

## BRING IT TOGETHER

**7** **a** Read the magazine article. Choose the correct options 1–3 to complete Antonia's message.

# Karim's Africa Questions

Dear Karim,
I (1)*'m traveling / will travel* to Mali next month. Before I (2)*leave / 'm leaving*, I want to find out more about the local cuisine. (3)*I'll be staying / I'll have stayed* in hotels and also with a local family.
Antonia

Antonia, your letter was delayed, so you'll already (4)________ arrived in Mali by the time my column appears—sorry! However, I hope that once you (5)________ read my reply, you'll know even more about Malian cuisine.

I expect that the family (6)________ cook a lot of meat dishes, like *yassa*. That's a spicy dish with onion and lemon. It's usually made with grilled chicken, (7)________ there is fish available. There's also *mafé*, beef boiled with peanuts. I have recipes for both and (8)________ be uploading them to the website by the end of the week.

*Couscous* is also popular. When I go home to Mali, my mother cooks it for me almost as soon as I (9)________ walked through the door! It's real comfort food. Also look for *Meni-meniyang*, a sticky honey, butter and sesame dessert. Once (10)________ tried that, you won't want any other dessert. It's delicious!
Karim

**b** Complete Karim's reply with one word in each blank 4–10 (*don't*, etc. = one word).

## FUNCTIONAL LANGUAGE Checking understanding

**1** **a** Complete the words to make a conversation.

A OK, we need to discuss what we have to do before we can open. George, have you looked into licensing?

B Sorry, (1)c______ you s______ that again?

A Licensing—we need to have a license before we can open.

B Oh, I've applied, and we should get a license next month.

C So am I (2)r______ in t______ that we can't open before that?

A No, we can't. But there's still plenty to do! We need to decorate, buy furniture and source ingredients. George! Are you (3)f______ ?

B Yes, sorry. (4)W______ you say "source ingredients," do you m______ buy food?

A Yes, we want to find the best ingredients at the lowest prices. We need to meet suppliers and check out the local markets.

B Can I just (5)c______ s______? Are we still planning to only buy food within 30 kilometers of here?

A Yes, that's going to be our USP, isn't it?

B What (6)e______ do you m______ by USP?

A "Unique selling point." It's what makes us special. Does that make (7)s______?

B Yes, completely. But what about drinks?

A Well, that's a little more difficult. If we have the same policy for drinks, we'll only be able to serve water and apple juice! Do you (8)s______ w______ I mean?

B Hmm, yes, I agree. One (9)t______ I don't u______, though, is who's going to do all the paperwork when we open. We'll all be so busy cooking and serving food.

A Good point, maybe we need to employ a manager...

**b** What business are the people in **1a** planning to start? Mark (✓) the correct picture.

a ☐

b ☐

c ☐

## LISTENING Recognizing context

**1** **a** 5.2 Listen to five short conversations. Who is speaking? Number speakers a–e in the order that you hear them.

a coworkers ___
b a tour guide and some tourists ___
c a family ___
d a taxi driver and a customer ___
e a waiter and a customer ___

**b** Listen again. Answer the questions.

1 What kind of food does the restaurant serve in conversation 1?
______________________________

2 What are the people going to eat in conversation 2?
______________________________

3 What drink does the woman order in conversation 3?
______________________________

4 What is the boy going to eat first and second in conversation 4?
______________________________

5 How does Zahra describe the chicken dish in conversation 5?
______________________________

**STRATEGY** When you listen to people talking, try to understand the general situation. Who are the people? Where are they? How do they know each other? This can help you understand what they are saying.

## READING Guessing unknown words

**1** Read "The Story of Cinnamon" and answer the questions.

1 Which island is mentioned in the text?

______________________

2 Which two uses of cinnamon are mentioned?

______________________

# *The Story of* Cinnamon

In the Indian Ocean, there is an island so beautiful that its ancient name, Serendeep, gave us the modern word *serendipity*—to find something wonderful by chance. This island of lush tropical jungles and heavy rains also hid a great secret for thousands of years, for it was the only source of one of the world's most precious spices, cinnamon. Today the island is known as Sri Lanka.

Cinnamon is first mentioned in Chinese writing from 2700 B.C. Yet despite its long use, its origin was obscure. Ancient thinkers guessed that cinnamon was caught in fishing nets by sailors on the Nile. It was an Arab philosopher who first surmised that it was a product of the East.

But what exactly is cinnamon? It's actually the bark of a tree. People take it off the outside of the tree and dry it on the ground where it curls up into tubes. Interestingly, today both plantation owners and workers share the profits of this trade. The workers get one-third of the sale price with the rest going to the landowner. Sharing the wealth encourages everyone to produce the best quality cinnamon.

Production of the spice is of enormous importance to Sri Lanka. Although it's no longer a luxury good, it is used in cooking worldwide. In the USA, people eat it with toast, or use it to bake cakes and cookies. In the Middle East it is added to roast lamb, and it is boiled with meat and vegetables in traditional Persian stews.

However, the future does not look rosy. It is difficult to find workers to harvest the crop. People have been leaving the plantations to move to the city, a trend that will be increasing over future years. Older workers fear that within a generation people will have forgotten the skills needed to prepare cinnamon. This is worrying as although the work is hard, producing cinnamon does pay well.

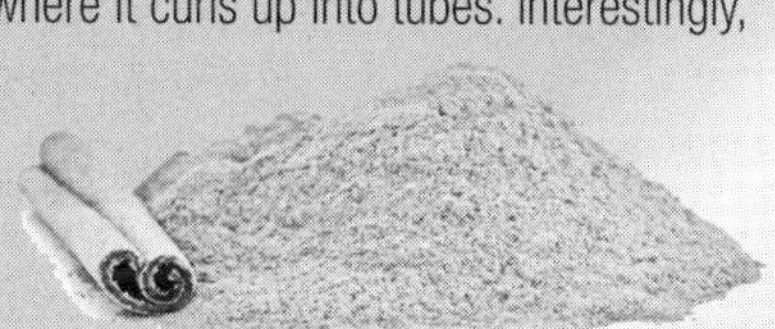

Perhaps all is not lost. Scientists are interested in the medicinal properties of cinnamon, and they will be experimenting with new ways of using it during next the few years. By the end of the decade, medicines based on cinnamon will have been developed to combat diabetes, and it will also have been used to help produce chemicals for cancer research. So it seems there are still chapters to be written in the 5,000-year history of cinnamon.

**2 a** Read the text again. Look at the underlined words. What kind of words are they? Can you guess their meaning just from the information around them?

**b** Match the underlined words in **2a** to definitions 1–7.

1 a kind of heavy soup made with vegetables, meat, fish, etc. ____________
2 the hard wooden "skin" on the outside of a tree ____________
3 the characteristics of a chemical or a substance ____________
4 to guess something or make a conclusion based on facts and information ____________
5 very green, with lots of plants ____________
6 something that is happy or good ____________
7 a farm (usually in a hot country) where bananas, sugar, etc. are grown ____________

**STRATEGY** When you read a text, you probably won't understand every word. When you see a word you don't know, try to guess the meaning from context. What kind of word is it (noun, verb, etc.)? Look at the words before and after it. Do they help you understand the meaning? If you took the word out of the sentence, what word would you use in your language?

# 6 THAT'S ENTERTAINMENT

## VOCABULARY
### Entertainment

**1** Complete the words.

**So Giovanna, why did you become a clown?**

For the money! No seriously, I used to work as a street (1)p _ _ f _ _ _ _ _ r, playing guitar in the street. I also did a little act as a (2)m _ m _ a _ t _ _ _ , you know, acting without words. One day a member of the (3)a _ d _ _ _ _ c _ told me that my act was really funny. He was a (4)m _ g _ _ i _ n doing tricks and illusions in the local circus—and he got me the job.

**What's the best thing about being a clown?**

Working with the other people. All the other circus (5)p _ _ f _ _ m _ _ s are really nice people. And the (6)m _ k _ u _ artist who does my face makes me laugh so much before I go on stage. She could be a (7)s _ _ _ d-u _ comedian if she wanted.

**What's the worst thing about being a clown?**

People don't take you seriously.

**Where do you see your career going?**

My dream is to be a (8)s _ _ _ _ tw _ _ t _ r in the movies. I am working on a story now about some wooden (9)p _ pp _ ts who come to life and run away from the circus. My boyfriend is a (10)s _ _ n _ e _ g _ n _ _ _ for TV here in Montevideo and he knows the right people, so maybe I can get a director or someone to read it.

**Well, we wish you the best of luck, Giovanna!**

**2** **a** Find ten movie and theater words in the word search.

| L | S | S | C | R | I | P | T | S | A |
|---|---|---|---|---|---|---|---|---|---|
| H | O | V | F | Q | Z | H | J | P | W |
| I | U | Y | Z | J | B | C | F | E | P |
| P | N | K | X | M | H | A | X | C | E |
| A | D | H | R | W | W | S | X | I | R |
| R | T | P | L | O | T | T | F | A | F |
| T | R | M | Q | M | V | Z | Z | L | O |
| R | A | B | S | C | E | N | E | E | R |
| E | C | A | F | Y | K | O | J | F | M |
| C | K | Z | S | T | A | G | E | F | A |
| O | S | C | E | N | E | R | Y | E | N |
| P | O | U | S | D | T | L | A | C | C |
| G | I | Q | L | P | O | R | W | T | E |
| V | D | M | E | B | T | T | S | S | L |

**b** Match the words from **2a** to the definitions. There are two words that you don't need.

1 Part of a movie or TV show where all the action happens in one place, like a chapter in a book. s_______
2 All the actors who are working on a play or a movie. c_______
3 The written words of a movie or TV series that the actors must learn. s_______
4 A role played by one actor in a movie or TV series. p_______
5 Amazing images or scenes in a movie, made with computers or models, etc. s_______ e_______
6 The story of a movie, book or play. p_______
7 All the music and songs in a movie. s_______
8 The place where the actors stand when they are acting in the theater. s_______

**3** Circle the word that doesn't work in each sentence.

1 I found this movie really *action-packed / memorable / moving*, even though its plot is very simple.
2 We felt great after watching this movie. It was really *hilarious / depressing / uplifting*.
3 This crime movie is really *gripping / intriguing / predictable*—you'll never guess how it ends!
4 I didn't enjoy the movie at all. I thought it was *unrealistic / hilarious / depressing*.
5 The start of the movie is really *action-packed / unrealistic / memorable*. I was very impressed by the first scene.

## Noun-building suffixes

**4** Complete the sentences with the noun form of the word in parentheses.

1 Making the movie wasn't a lot of fun because there was a lot of _______ between the cast and the director. (tense)
2 She's a great actress, but she has one _______ : she's not very good at comedy. (weak)
3 The new science fiction movie is creating a lot of _______ at the moment. (excite)
4 Is there a movie theater in this _______ ? (neighbor)
5 You need a lot of _______ to be a successful stage set designer. (create)
6 I loved Japanese cartoons in my _______. (child)
7 The plot is very hard to follow; it caused a lot of _______ in the audience! (confuse)

## Computer games

**5** Choose the correct options to complete the text.

Nowadays every [(1)] *first / one* person game seems to be based on killing, so you'd think the most popular computer games character would be some soldier from a violent [(2)] *gun / shoot* 'em up. In fact, it's a friendly Italian plumber called Mario, Nintendo's megastar.

Mario first appeared in a classic [(3)] *platform / station* game for arcades: *Donkey Kong*. In the game, players [(4)] *go / make* up a level after dodging barrels thrown at them by a giant ape. It was completely addictive as people progressed from one [(5)] *ladder / stage* to the next. Its simple [(6)] *drawings / graphics* explain Mario's distinctive red and blue costume: those bright colors made him easier to see.

Mario is popular with children as well as adults, so he's often the star in each new Nintendo [(7)] *apparatus / console*, like the Wii. One of their biggest sellers was 2008's *Super Mario Kart*, where players race on a [(8)] *divided / split* screen. The game's innovation was its steering wheel: players slot their handheld [(9)] *controller / remote* into the back of it. Then the machine can [(10)] *"look"/"read"* their movements using sophisticated motion [(11)] *alarms / sensors*, just like they're driving a car. Nintendo fans agree that the Mario games have always provided excellent [(12)] *gameplay / game pleasure*, from the birth of the Mario character in 1981, right up to the present day!

## Vocabulary Extension

### Further noun forms

**6** **a** Complete the chart with ten movie and theater jobs. Add the suffixes in the table to the root words in the box.

~~act~~ cartoon comedy compose criticize
direct drama illustrate music produce

| -ian | -er/-or | -ist | -ic |
|---|---|---|---|
| | *actor* | | |

**b** 6.1 Listen and check.

**7** Complete the sentences with the correct form of nouns from **6a**.

1 The play was very popular with the public, but the _______ didn't like it.
2 George is so funny; he really should be a(n) _______ .
3 Writing music is tough—not many _______ make a living from it.
4 Someone who writes plays is known as a(n) _______ .
5 You have to be good at drawing to be a(n) _______ or a(n) _______ .
6 Some people think that the _______ and the _______ of a movie are more important than the cast.

## Bring It Together

**8** Complete the e-mail with the words from the box. There is one word that you don't need.

actor audience circus console controllers critic
hilarious magician neighborhood part script

Hi Jim!

How are you doing? I'm writing to tell you about Anna's play. It was an amazing success. There were about 200 people in the [(1)] _______ — I think almost everyone in the [(2)] _______ had decided to come and see it. There was even a theater [(3)] _______ from the regional paper!

Anna wrote the [(4)] _______ and she directed the play, too. It's about a group of [(5)] _______ performers and their lives as they travel around the country. The [(6)] _______ is getting older, and he's losing his ability to do tricks and illusions. At the same time, a young puppeteer is becoming really successful because his part of the show is [(7)] _______ —people find his act really funny, and the magician is jealous. I played one of the clowns from the circus. It was a small [(8)] _______ but a lot of fun.

There was only one problem on the night when I was supposed to be playing on a games [(9)] _______ with another character. They had forgotten to put the [(10)] _______ on the stage, so we had nothing in our hands! We just carried on, and I don't think anyone noticed—I hope not, anyway!

If you want to see some photos, they're up on our website. I bet my clown costume will make you laugh!

Talk soon, Natalia

## GRAMMAR
### The passive voice

**1** Put the words in the correct order to make sentences.

1 in / play / the / set / is / Thailand

______________________

2 be / month / the / released / will / next / movie

______________________

3 Hitchcock / by / directed / was / movie / the

______________________

4 the / was / Cruz / role / for / starring / Penelope / chosen

______________________

5 being / by / Clooney / written / George / script / the / is

______________________

6 been / the / given / TV / has / show / reviews / great

______________________

**2** **a** Rewrite these sentences, as in the example. The first word is given.

1 They chose Clint Eastwood for the lead role in *A Fistful of Dollars.*
Clint Eastwood *was chosen for the lead role in A Fistful of Dollars.*

2 They use Glasgow as the setting for a lot of movies nowadays.
Glasgow ______________________.

3 Many people think that *Citizen Kane* is the best movie of all time.
It ______________________.

4 People say that you can see a modern plane in the 1963 movie *Cleopatra*.
It ______________________.

5 The Japanese company Studio Ghibli made the movie *Spirited Away*.
*Spirited Away* ______________________.

6 In the 1920s, people thought it was impossible to make color movies.
In the 1920s, it ______________________.

7 Many countries banned the movie *A Clockwork Orange*.
The movie ______________________.

8 They believe that saying the name of the play *Macbeth* is unlucky in theater.
It ______________________.

**b** Which sentences in **2a** refer to

i facts? __________

ii opinions? __________

**3** Correct the sentences. Mark (✓) two correct sentences.

1 We were told that the movie was sold out.
2 The play has been received a lot of praise.
3 I have invited to the premiere of the latest Tom Cruise movie.
4 The song was written of Paul McCartney.
5 The part of Sherlock Holmes is be played by Benedict Cumberbatch.
6 The performance is going to be cancel due to bad weather.
7 It is think that people will stop buying DVDs in the future.
8 A scene from the movie is being shot in the City Museum today.

**4** Complete the text with the correct passive form of the verbs in parentheses.

**Spotlight on... Hong Kong Movies**

For many years now, the Hong Kong movie industry (1)________ (know) for its martial arts films and exciting action movies. It (2)________ (also / admire) for a long time for its output: in 2009, over fifty movies (3)________ (produce). However, the Hong Kong movie industry is now getting a new kind of recognition. In 2008, American movie *The Departed* won the Best Picture Oscar. The movie (4)________ (base) on a 2002 Hong Kong hit, *Infernal Affairs*. The remake was a double success for director Martin Scorsese, who finally picked up the Best Director Oscar after he (5)________ (beat) to the award several times before. Suddenly, everyone was talking about Hong Kong movies.

It (6)________ (think) that the local movie industry will continue to grow in the future. Foreign interest in Hong Kong movies (7)________ (encourage) by the recent international success of superstars like Chow Yun-Fat, who appears in 2012's *The Monkey King*. Nowadays, local moviemakers (8)________ (give) more and more government funding: with its combination of talent, energy and government support, it's clear that Hong Kong will be one of the places to watch over the next few years. You heard it here first!

## Have something done

**5** Match a–b to i–ii.

1 a The circus performers had their tent put up ____
  b The circus performers put their tent up ____
  i by themselves because it was a small circus company.
  ii by a team who worked for them.
2 a The composer recorded his new song ____
  b The composer got his song recorded ____
  i by a professional sound engineer.
  ii using his own equipment.
3 a The director had the script rewritten ____
  b The director rewrote the script ____
  i by a new scriptwriter.
  ii without anybody's help.
4 a We're a small theater, so the actors put ____
  b On a movie set, the actors have their makeup put ____
  i on by a makeup artist.
  ii on their own makeup.
5 a Simon translated his play into Chinese ____
  b Simon had his play translated into Chinese ____
  i by a writer from Guangzhou.
  ii by using a dictionary and the Internet.
6 a He got the scenery built ____
  b He built the scenery ____
  i by a team of backstage workers.
  ii himself to save money.

**6** **a** Write sentences using the correct form of the verb in parentheses.

1 I / have / my red carpet dresses / by top designers (make)
______________________________

2 I / have / special shoes / to me / from Paris (send)
______________________________

3 I / always / have / my face / white / before / I go / on stage (paint)
______________________________

4 I / have / silk scarves, flowers and a rabbit / to me / before my act (bring)
______________________________

5 I / have / had / my reviews / in national newspapers (publish)
______________________________

**b** Who do you think said the sentences in **6a**? Match them to the people.

a a magician ____________
b a movie star ____________
c a theater critic ____________
d a mime artist ____________
e a ballerina ____________

## Bring It Together

**7** Complete the text with one word in each blank (*don't*, etc. = one word).

### Kite Crazy in Afghanistan

Today, the skies above Kabul (1)______ filled with hundreds of colorful papers. It's autumn and Afghanistan's kite-flying season has just begun. For many years, kite flying had (2)______ banned, and it has only recently (3)______ permitted again, which is great news for its followers. Even during the ban, kites (4)______ being produced secretly in hidden workshops, but now real stores (5)______ being opened again all over the city. That's not surprising because kite flying is an Afghan obsession. A kite is flown (6)______ two people: one controlling the string and the other the movement of the kite. They (7)______ used in contests like 'kite fighting' where players try to cut the string of the other person's kite. If they succeed, and the string gets (8)______ , the kite flies away into the air. These kites can (9)______ claimed by anyone in the city. That's OK because most of them are very cheap, although some serious players (10)______ their kite specially made by experts. Whoever makes them, the kites almost always have bright, dynamic designs—and some people hang them on the walls as decorations!

## FUNCTIONAL LANGUAGE Generalizing

**1** Complete the words in the conversations.

1 A What kind of people take the course in moviemaking?
B Well, a __ a r ___ e, people already have some experience in the movie industry, but it's not essential.

2 A How does your group find gigs?
B What o ___ n h ___ p ___ s is that we go to concerts, and then we ask the people there if they are interested in hearing our band.

3 A How often do you use the games console?
B We only use it when we have parties, g ___ r ___ y s ___ k ___ g. We don't play the games on our own much.

4 A Why do people take up salsa dancing as a hobby?
B M __ r __ o __ t ___ t ___ n n ___, people just do it because it's fun and a good way to stay in shape.

5 A How do you meet people who do the same hobby as you—making animated movies?
B I __'s o __ t ___ the c __ s __ that I've run into them at conferences and fairs. There are always loads of other animators there.

6 A Do people often get hurt performing these circus tricks?
B Oh no. I __ m __ s __ c __ s __ s, people are really careful. Accidents are very rare.

## LISTENING Intonation

**1** 6.2 Listen to two conversations. Mark (✓) 1, 2 or both.

| In which conversation | 1 | 2 | both |
|---|---|---|---|
| a do the speakers know each other well? | | | |
| b has someone lost something? | | | |
| c do they talk about a movie? | | | |
| d do they talk about a game? | | | |
| e do they talk about making things? | | | |

**2 a** Look at sentences 1–6. Which conversation are they from? Write 1 or 2.

a ☐ That must be really hard on you. ↗/↘
b ☐ It's a great movie. ↗/↘
c ☐ They're beautiful! ↗/↘
d ☐ I'd love to give it a try! ↗/↘
e ☐ I'm really sorry, but I can't. ↗/↘
f ☐ It would be awful if you didn't have it. ↗/↘

**b** Read the information in the Strategy box. Do you think the speaker will use rising (↗) or falling (↘) intonation in the sentences? Circle the correct answers.

**3 a** Listen again and check your answers in **2**.

**b** In which conversation is one of the speakers not saying exactly what he/she means? How do you know?

**STRATEGY** When you listen, think about how a speaker says something (their intonation) as well as what he/she says.

- When people feel happy or enthusiastic about something, they usually use rising (↗) intonation.
- When they express sympathy about something, they usually use falling (↘) intonation.
- Remember that sometimes people don't say exactly what they mean, perhaps because they are trying to be polite or to make a joke. In this case, instead of rising or falling, their intonation often remains flat.

## WRITING Summarizing a plot

### *The Year of the Hare (Jäniksen vuosi)*
by Arto Paasilinna

*The Year of the Hare* is a novel by Finnish author Arto Paasilinna. It's set in modern-day Finland, in both the capital Helsinki and the country's deep, northern forests. It's a heartwarming tale about Vatanen, a journalist, whose whole life changes after an encounter with a wild hare.

When the story opens, Vatanen is traveling with a photographer colleague. One night, they hit a hare with their car. The injured animal escapes into the forest, and when Vatanen goes to look for it, the photographer drives off, leaving him alone.

While Vatanen is taking care of the frightened and injured hare, he makes an important decision. He decides to leave his hectic life in the city and travel the country with the animal as his companion. Following the news that he will not be returning to work, his wife and colleagues come to look for him. However, Vatanen refuses to return to his previous life. Instead, he begins an extraordinary road trip towards the Arctic Circle, always traveling with the hare by his side. His adventures include encounters with wild bears and forest fires as well as an accidental trip into Russian territory.

The main character, Vatanen, is middle-aged and depressed. He is tired of writing unmemorable lifestyle articles for magazines and wants to taste real freedom. As he meets the people who live in the forests, like park rangers and farmers, he discovers that life has meaning all over again.

Combining a road trip with a story of personal discovery, *The Year of the Hare* is a pleasant story about how people can change direction and return to a simpler, more natural way of life.

**1** Read the plot summary quickly. Mark (✓) the information that it contains.

- ☐ the beginning of the story
- ☐ the end of the story
- ☐ where the story happens
- ☐ the names of all the characters
- ☐ the main events of the story
- ☐ the writer's opinion of the story
- ☐ a physical description of the main character
- ☐ the main theme/idea of the book

**2** Complete the phrases. Then check your answers in the text.

1 It's s______ in modern-day Finland
2 It's a heartwarming t______ about
3 When the story o______
4 W______ Vatanen is taking care of the frightened and injured hare
5 F______ the news that he will not be returning to work
6 His a______ include encounters with wild bears and forest fires
7 C______ a road trip with a story of personal discovery

**STRATEGY** When you write a plot summary of a book or a movie:

- use the present simple to summarize the main events of the story
- don't include all the events of the story. Focus on one or two key scenes
- use sequencing expressions (e.g., *first*, *while*, *following*) to show the order of events
- only describe one or two main characters. Concentrate on their personality and don't include physical description
- in your conclusion, summarize the main themes or "big ideas" of the story.

**3** Write a plot summary of a book or a movie that you know well. Use the paragraph plan to help you.

*Paragraph 1: Where/When is it set? Who is the main character?*

*Paragraph 2: How does the story begin? What is the most important event in the book?*

*Paragraph 3: describe one or two additional events*

*Paragraph 4: describe the main character's personality*

*Paragraph 5: conclusion—explain the main theme*

# PROGRESS TEST 2

## GRAMMAR & VOCABULARY (25 points)

**1** Complete the sentences with the correct form of the word in parentheses. *(10 points)*

0 I have *known* (know) Ximena for over five years now.
1 Don't send that e-mail! I _________ (finish) writing it yet!
2 It's time you came out of the water and had something to eat. You _________ (swim) for hours now!
3 Everyone's looking forward to _________ (see) you when you visit next month.
4 Walter can't take the exam unless he _________ (register) online.
5 Read the sign; no _________ (eat) in the computer room.
6 We're in a taxi, but the traffic's not moving. We _________ (miss) our flight!
7 By the end of the month, you _________ (work) here for ten years.
8 I had my wallet _________ (steal) at the train station.
9 It _________ (believe) that there are many undiscovered animal species in the ocean.
10 Once Clarissa _________ (read) your report, she'll want to ask you about it.

**2** Circle the option that doesn't work. *(7 points)*

0 I love your *bald* / *dark* / *wavy* hair!
1 Zack looks completely different now that he's grown a *beard* / *complexion* / *mustache*.
2 Do you think Sofia has put on *freckles* / *makeup* / *weight*?
3 The pictures in the book were drawn by a(n) *cartoonist* / *illustrator* / *producer*.
4 I like to use herbs like *coriander* / *cinnamon* / *basil* in my cooking.
5 Apples taste best when they're *crunchy* / *sweet* / *creamy* and juicy.
6 The movie was terrible. It was really *intriguing* / *predictable* / *unrealistic*.
7 I felt sad at the end of the play because it was so *depressing* / *gripping* / *moving*.

**3** Read the definitions. Write the correct words. *(8 points)*

0 This describes a movie that makes you feel very happy and positive at the end. u*plifting*
1 These are lines on your face that you get as you become older. w_________
2 This verb means to cook in very hot water. b_________
3 This word can be used to describe the taste of coffee or lemon. b_________
4 You eat with these two pieces of wood in many parts of the world. c_________
5 This is a company that does business in many different countries. m_________
6 This is a musician who performs on the street. S_________ p_________
7 This is the story of what happens in a book, movie, play, opera, etc. e_________
8 This is the time in your life between being a baby and a teenager. c_________

## READING (25 points)

**1** Read the text on page 41 and find five jobs that Tom Shadyac has done in the entertainment business. *(5 points)*

_________ _________ _________
_________ _________

**2** Correct six mistakes in this summary of the article. *(6 points)*

*After directing a series of unsuccessful movies, Tom Shadyac decided to change his life. He sold his apartment in Hollywood and moved into a trailer and started to give his money away to people on the street. Nowadays, he thinks no one's work is important in the movies, so he has completely changed his outlook on life. He astonished the host of The Oprah Winfrey Show with his story, but he says he has no regrets and is now a student at a university in Southern California.*

**3** Answer the questions about the article. *(14 points)*

1 Which movie stars has Tom Shadyac worked with?
_________________________
2 What kinds of movies has Shadyac made?
_________________________
3 What event made him change his life?
_________________________
4 What kind of people appear in *I am?*
_________________________
5 What TV shows did he appear on?
_________________________
6 What skill does he now teach other people?
_________________________
7 How does Shadyac feel since he gave away his fortune?
_________________________

## I Am Tom Shadyac...

Imagine you were a Hollywood movie director, responsible for hit movies like *Patch Adams* (with Robin Williams in the lead role) or *The Nutty Professor* (starring Eddie Murphy). What would you do next? Probably not what Tom Shadyac did. He sold his Hollywood mansion and most of his possessions and moved into a trailer (a simple kind of mobile home). He gave it all up to live a simple life and then made a movie of his experiences, *I am* (2011).

This documentary tells how Shadyac chose a new direction in life after he was badly hurt in a bicycle accident. It convinced him to give up the pressure of his Hollywood life.

*I am* shows his interviews with various gurus and philosophers, such as Noam Chomsky, as he tries to find the meaning of life. For Shadyac, this means showing respect to everyone. He says now that as the director of a movie, his role is no more important than anyone else from the sound engineer to the cleaner. Everyone's work is important.

This is very different to the usual way of thinking in the movie business, but Shadyac has more surprises, too. Earlier this year, he astonished the audience on *The Oprah Winfrey Show* by telling them that he had given away most of his fortune to charity.

Shadyac is one of those people who is successful at everything he does. Once he earned his degree from UCLA Film School, he was quickly identified as a future talent. He began his career as an actor, working on small-screen shows like *Magnum PI*. Later, he moved into directing and also became a producer of his latest movies.

As a moviemaker his specialty is humor, something he developed as a stand-up comedian early in his career. This has also been useful when he has taken on the role of scriptwriter on his projects such as *Ace Ventura*, starring world-famous Jim Carrey. That's one part of his life that he hasn't given up as he now instructs people on how to write top-quality scripts at Pepperdine University in Southern California.

Despite giving up all that money, Shadyac insists he is happier now than he ever was when he was at the top of the Hollywood tree.

## LISTENING *(25 points)*

**1** T2 Listen to a podcast about a computer game, *Cooking Mama World Kitchen*. Mark (✓) the things that are mentioned. *(9 points)*

| | | |
|---|---|---|
| ☐ console | ☐ controller | ☐ first person |
| ☐ the gameplay | ☐ characters | ☐ graphics |
| ☐ platform | ☐ motion sensor | ☐ shoot 'em up |

**2** Listen again. Are the sentences true (T) or false (F)? Correct the false sentences. *(16 points)*

1 *Cooking Mama World Kitchen* was invented in 2011 for the Nintendo DS. T / F

______________________________

2 You can cut ingredients with a knife as part of the game. T / F

______________________________

3 On the podcast, they talk about frying and grilling ingredients. T / F

______________________________

4 *Cooking Mama* now offers 3D gameplay. T / F

______________________________

5 Jake thinks that the character of Mama is too serious. T / F

______________________________

6 Jake made some cookies using a recipe from *Cooking Mama*. T / F

______________________________

7 Leila's hamburger was eaten by Mama. T / F

______________________________

8 Leila thinks *Cooking Mama* is a good game to play by yourself. T / F

______________________________

## WRITING *(25 points)*

**1** Complete the words in the e-mail. *(5 points)*

Hi Alessandra
(0) *H o w* are you? (1) G __ __ s __ who I met the other day! Tanja, from our old jewelry-making course, remember? I hadn't seen her (2) s __ __ __ __ the end of the course. I can't (3) b __ __ i __ __ __ how much she's changed!
She's (4) s __ __ __ l really thin, but she now has dyed red hair. And she wears this amazing handmade jewelry, too. She has a really individual (5) __ __ __ k. I took our picture with my phone (I've attached it to this e-mail). Check out her web page online; she's now working as a makeup artist in the movie industry!
Bye for now,
Kim

**2** You meet an old classmate that you haven't seen for a long time. Your classmate has completely changed his/her appearance and job. Write an e-mail to a friend telling them about him/her. *(20 points)*

### 1.1, *p. 3, Ex 6*

1 It was typical! It was about ten years ago, and we were going on vacation in the car. We set out really early in the morning, at about 5 a.m. We picked up my cousin at her house, and then we set out on our trip to the beach. It was a really sunny day and everyone was in a good mood when, suddenly, the car broke down! It just stopped... right in the middle of nowhere! It was awful. Dad thought he could straighten the problem out, but it was too difficult for him to fix. So, we had to call for help. When the mechanic came, he said the car was in really bad shape and he needed two weeks to repair it. So we just gave up and went home. My mom was really unhappy. I don't think she spoke to my dad for a week!

2 Once, I was working in the university library with my friends. We were under a lot of pressure because we had to turn in a big project later that day. Suddenly, the fire alarm went off. At first, we just ignored it. The university tests the fire alarms at 3 p.m. every Wednesday, so we went on working as usual. I was just writing down the last part of the report when a security guard came in and shouted at us to leave the building. There really was a fire—at 3 p.m. on Wednesday! Apparently, someone threw a cigarette away while it was still lit and some paper in the trash can caught on fire.

### 1.2, *p. 6, Exs 1 & 2*

1 **A:** Hello. I'm Nick.
**B:** Julieta. Nice to meet you, Nick.
**A:** Are you with the bride or the groom, Julieta?
**B:** I know the bride, Vera. She's my best friend, in fact!
**A:** OK. So, how did you meet?
**B:** We studied Spanish together in Buenos Aires. As a matter of fact, I have a photo of us. Would you like to see it?
**A:** Sure.
**B:** Look! Here we are with our classmates, there were twelve of us altogether. That's me on the left. And Vera is here.
**A:** Oh yeah. I see her. It's a great picture.
**B:** Thanks. So are you a friend of Dan, the groom?
**A:** Yes, I am. I'm a friend of the family. I've known Dan since he was a baby.
**B:** And now you're here at the wedding! That's so nice. Where are you from, Nick?
**A:** Canada. I just flew in to Boston yesterday.
**B:** Really? I think you brought the cold weather with you. It's freezing today! It must be about two degrees out there.
**A:** Hmm, well, it was –10 at home in Ottawa when I left!

2 **C:** Paula! Welcome to Hong Kong! It's so good to see you! How was the flight?
**D:** Not bad, thanks. I feel exhausted now though!
**C:** Yeah, I bet. Did you manage to sleep on the plane?
**D:** Well, a little, but a funny thing happened. I found my seat on the plane, sat down. Then I glanced over at the row next to me, and I realized that the person sitting there was Michaela, you know, from my old office!
**C:** You're joking! Really? You were pretty close friends, weren't you? She's the girl with the curly hair, isn't she?
**D:** Yes, she is. It was such a coincidence! We spent most of the flight talking, catching up on each other's news.
**C:** So what is she doing at the moment?
**D:** Well, she was studying for a degree in business administration, but she dropped out. She didn't like it because she didn't get along well with her classmates.
**C:** Oh, that's a shame. Anyway, let me take your bag. You can tell me the rest of your news in the car.

### 2.1, *p. 12, Ex 1*

**A:** Hello, welcome to Park Lane Clinic. How can I help you?
**B:** Oh, hello. My name's Jennifer Chan. I wonder if you could give me some advice. I'm traveling to India next month. Could you tell me if I need any vaccinations?
**A:** Certainly. One moment, please. Right, it says here that you'll need two different injections.
**B:** OK. Would it be possible to get the vaccinations here in the clinic?
**A:** Yes, but you'll have to make an appointment with Dr. Green. She's available on Monday, Wednesday and Thursday afternoon.
**B:** OK... Do you have any idea how long the appointment will take?
**A:** Uh, it'll take about 20 minutes. There are appointments available at 2 p.m. and 4:35 on Thursday. Would either of those work?
**B:** Yes, I'll come at 4:35. Would you mind writing that on a card for me? I don't have my day planner, and I'll probably forget otherwise!
**A:** Of course, here you are. We'll see you on Thursday, October 12 at 4:35.
**B:** Great. Thanks very much for your help.

### 2.2, *p. 12, Ex 1 & 2*

**A:** Today in *Ask the Expert*, we're with top vet Alexandra Haynes. Our first caller is Gina Truman from Birmingham. What's your question, Gina?
**B:** Hello?
**C:** Hi, Gina.
**B:** Well, I want to become a vet when I graduate. I wonder if you could give me some advice about studying veterinary science.
**C:** OK, well, there are many different kinds of vets. A lot of vets work with small animals family pets, like hamsters and cats. Other vets work on farms with animals like sheep, horses and so on. I used to work on a dairy farm. I learned a lot about working with large animals. That's very useful in my current job, at a safari park. I work with a lot of exotic animals these days!
**B:** I think I'd like to work with horses.
**C:** Fantastic. There are lots of jobs in that area. Uh... How old are you, Gina?
**B:** 16.
**C:** Great. Whatever you do, choose the right school subjects next year. If you want to major in veterinary science in college, you should study biology, chemistry and math.
**B:** Oh, OK... Well, math isn't my best subject, but I really like science. My highest grades are always in biology!
**C:** That's good. And I guess you really like animals?
**B:** Yes, I do. I love horseback riding. I ride at a local farm about four times a week. I'm also doing some volunteer work at an animal shelter near my home. We take care of dogs without owners.
**C:** Perfect. Universities want to know that you have hands-on experience working with animals. Volunteering is an excellent idea.
**B:** Great!
**C:** Now, the other thing I should tell you is that veterinary work can be hard. The hours aren't really a problem; they can be long, but you'll quickly get used to that. No, you need to be prepared to see some very badly injured animals. Sometimes, you have to decide if an animal will live or die. It's important to be tough as well as kind.
**B:** I think I can do that.
**A:** Any last words of advice, Alexandra?
**C:** Mm, yes. It takes five years of college to become a vet; that's a lot of studying! Courses can be very expensive, especially because you'll need to travel around the country to get work experience. If I were you, I'd talk to someone about money before you start college, maybe a family member, or someone from your bank. You don't want to have to drop out because you can't afford it.

**A:** OK, Alexandra, thank you very much. Gina, has that answered your questions?
**B:** Yes, definitely. Thank you.
**C:** My pleasure. Good luck, Gina!

### 3.2, *p. 18, Exs 1 & 2*

And now for an update on tomorrow's weather. There will be very mixed conditions across the country, including two severe weather warnings. Our first warning is for Cape Town, where there will be dense fog in the early morning. Visibility will be poor for many people in the region, so please drive carefully. Farther down the coast, in Port Elizabeth, there will be heavy rain throughout the day. In Durban, however, conditions are much brighter: there will be clear skies and warm weather all day long.
Inland, it's a very different story. Here in Pretoria, temperatures will drop overnight, and it will be cold and icy all morning. There's a low of –1ºC, but it will be warmer in the afternoon, with temperatures reaching 12 degrees in some areas. We could also see some light hail at about 3 or 4 o'clock. In the capital, Johannesburg, it will be a warmer day, but thunder and lightning are likely during the early afternoon. Last, we have a second severe weather warning for the Drakensberg Mountains. We expect blizzards and there could be large snowdrifts in some areas. Keep an eye on our website for updates on that if you are thinking of traveling through the mountains tomorrow. That's all from me for now. We'll be back for another weather update at 10 p.m.

### T1, *p. 21, Exs 1 & 2*

1 **A:** Hello.
**B:** Hello ... it's Amy, isn't it? From the German course?
**A:** That's right. Hi, Barry. I haven't seen you in ages.
**B:** No, I haven't been going to class because I've been really busy.
**A:** So what are you doing here?
**B:** Ah well, I'm going on a sailing trip next week, and I need to get a GPS for my boat. This is the best store in the city. Are you interested in sailing, too?
**A:** I am, yeah. I come to this store all the time. They have everything.
**B:** Yeah, they do. Well, I'll see you later.
**A:** Nice to see you. Bye!

2 **C:** OK, now just relax, dear. We're here.
**D:** Hurry. I think the baby's going to come at any moment.
**C:** It's all OK. Look, the nurses are all ready for you. Oh, and it's Janet who will be delivering the baby. That's good news, isn't it?
**D:** Janet... She delivered Mike and Charlie. She's delivered all our kids...
**C:** Yeah, so it's OK... Everything's under control.
**D:** Carlton... I'm so glad I married you.
**C:** I love you, too, darling. Now just stay calm. We'll get through this.

3 **E:** Miriam, may I have a word?
**F:** Sure, Lee. What's up?
**E:** I'm just preparing the conference room for the meeting with our new clients.
**F:** Uh-huh.
**E:** It's just... I know the meeting is important, but I'm not feeling well.
**F:** Oh. What's wrong?
**E:** I had a vaccination yesterday, and I've been feeling sick all day.
**F:** Well, you go home and rest. I'll take care of the meeting.
**E:** Oh, thanks Miriam.
**F:** Would you like a glass of water or something? You look very pale.

4 **G:** Excuse me! Hello!
**H:** Yes?
**G:** Hi. I wonder if you can help me. We're trying to find the amusement park.
**H:** Ah... You're in the wrong part of town. You need to drive down this street...
**G:** Yes...
**H:** And then take North Road. It's the third left, I think.
**G:** Is it a long way away?
**H:** Maybe another five kilometers.
**G:** Thank you very much for your help!
**H:** No problem. Enjoy yourselves!

5 **I:** I can't believe that we lost that match!
**J:** They just played better than us. Forget it, we have another game tomorrow. What do you want to eat—one of these sandwiches? Don't worry. I'll pay.
**J:** Er, yeah, OK. Thanks. And some orange juice, please. You know, I think we should have won the match. Harry and Pamela haven't been playing as long as we have.
**I:** But they never give up. They keep trying to win, right up to the end.
**J:** Mm, well, I suppose you're right. Thanks for this, by the way.
**I:** That's OK. I have to do something for my tennis partner, don't I!

### 4.1, *p. 26, Exs 1 & 2*

**A:** So, Chris, tell us about your work here in Macao...First of all, how did you become a tattooist?
**B:** Well, it's simple, really. My father and my grandfather were both tattoo artists, so it's kind of a family business... I say tattoo artist because tattooing is a real art. You need talent and patience, you know, like any artist.
**A:** And are tattoos very popular here?
**B:** Yes, they've been becoming more popular in recent years, but... they're still kind of controversial. In the past, many people associated tattoos with criminals and thought they were a bad thing. Even today, if you go on a job interview or something, you might need to cover up your tattoo... Obviously, I really like tattoos, though, all the different styles and designs...
**A:** Yeah, of course. Is there anything you dislike about your job, though?
**B:** Well... sometimes dealing with clients is difficult. Often people come and ask for a particular tattoo, but they haven't really thought about what they want. Just this morning I spoke to a guy about his tattoo design, and he changed his mind twice while he was talking to me! I refuse to tattoo people if they don't know exactly what they want.
**A:** Hmm, that makes sense. Do you do a lot of different designs?
**B:** Yeah, definitely.
**A:** And which are the most popular?
**B:** Mmm, many people want Chinese characters. And animal tattoos are very popular at the moment, too. In Chinese tradition, these animals have special meanings. A tattoo of a rabbit represents luck, for example. A tattoo of a monkey represents a fun or a lively person.
**A:** Right. I guess tattoos often say something about a person's character or identity...
**B:** Yeah, I think so. Tattoos are a form of expression. And I enjoy helping people change their look... I see myself as part of a tradition going back thousands of years and, you know, that makes me feel proud.
**A:** Well, thanks Chris, for talking to me about your work. It's been really interesting to find out...

### 5.2, *p. 32, Ex 1*

1 **A:** Where to then?
**B:** Well, we don't actually know. Do you know anywhere good to eat around here?
**A:** Well, yes. I could take you to Brick Lane. Do you like spicy food?
**B:** Yes, I do. Very much.
**A:** I can take you to a great restaurant. It serves the best Bangladeshi food you've ever eaten.
**B:** That sounds perfect! Let's go there, then.
**A:** We're on our wy.

2 **C:** Time for a break?
**D:** Yeah. I'm exhausted! I don't know how we're going to get this presentation done in time for the board meeting. We'll be working on it all night!
**C:** Well let's take a fifteen-minute break. I really need some coffee! Mmm... and one of those chocolate donuts from the cafeteria...
**D:** Yeah, I'm really hungry! Let's go then.

3 **E:** May I take your order?
**F:** Yes. I'd like the vegetarian lasagna, please.
**E:** Good choice. It comes with salad or french fries.
**F:** Oh, salad, please.
**E:** And to drink?
**F:** Just water.
**E:** Natural or sparkling?
**F:** Um... sparkling.
**E:** Perfect. It'll be about 15 minutes, OK?

4 **G:** Mm, they have ice cream! Can I have an ice cream?
**H:** Not until you've had your main course.
**G:** But I want ice cream!
**H:** Yes, and you can have some dessert once you've eaten your vegetables.
**G:** Oh, but...
**H:** William...
**G:** Oh all right.

5 **I:** Ladies and gentlemen. We've all had a busy morning, so we'll break for lunch now. After lunch, we'll continue looking around the old town.
**J:** Thanks Zahra, that was a lovely morning. The city is extraordinary... And this restaurant looks great, too. What do you recommend for lunch?
**I:** I'll be having the chicken couscous. It's very good here.
**J:** What's it like?
**I:** It's cooked with apricots and cinnamon, so it tastes sweet and it's very mild. Try it!
**J:** Mm, I think I will.

### 6.1, *p. 35, Ex 6*

I-A-N—comedian, musician
E-R, O-R—actor, composer, director, illustrator, producer
I-S-T—cartoonist, dramatist
I-C—critic

### 6.2, *p. 38, Exs 1–3*

1 **A:** Oh no!
**B:** What's wrong, Lucy?
**A:** I don't know where my DVD of *Twilight* is...
**B:** *Twilight?*
**A:** Yeah, you know, the vampire movie? With Robert Pattinson. You know the one.
**B:** Yeah, of course I know it. It's a great movie.
**A:** Well, I really need to find it. Monika's coming over this evening, and I promised her that we'd watch it.
**B:** Oh, OK, yeah. It would be awful if you didn't have it.
**A:** It must be here somewhere ...
**B:** You have so many DVDs, Lucy. Isn't there something else you could watch?
**A:** Not really. Monika really wants to see *Twilight*.
**B:** Mmm, well, it is a timeless classic.
**A:** Finally! Here it is! Hey, Carrie, why don't you join us tonight? We're just going to relax and watch the movie.
**B:** Oh, I'm really sorry, but I can't. I have lots to do. But thanks, Lucy.

2 **C:** Have you seen this photo, Jose?
**D:** Dominoes in Cuba! That takes me back.
**C:** And these guys playing it are young, too. They're our age.
**D:** People play it all the time back in Cuba. They're very competitive. They play really fast and they keep saying, "Come on, come on, it's not chess!"
**C:** Do you miss Cuba?
**D:** Yeah. I haven't been there for years.
**C:** That must be really hard on you. But I'm sure you'll go back there one day.
**D:** Yeah, well ,... Let me show you these... my dominoes.
**C:** Oh wow. They're beautiful! Are they handmade?
**D:** Yeah. I carved them myself. I love doing this kind of woodwork, in my spare time.
**C:** Well you're a real artist, Jose. These look as if they were made by a professional.
**D:** Thanks. So shall we play?
**C:** Sure, yeah. I'd love to give it a try!
**D:** OK, great. But I warn you, I'm very competitive!

### T2, *p. 41, Exs 1 & 2*

**A:** Hello. I'm Jake.
**B:** And I'm Leila. Welcome to our podcast. Every week we take a look at computer games that interest us. And this week, it's...
**A:** *Cooking Mama World Kitchen*. Leila, give us the background.
**B:** Cooking Mama is part of a series of games. The first one came out in 2006 for the Nintendo DS console, and the latest version is *Cooking Mama World Kitchen* for the Wii.
**A:** So what's special about the Wii version?
**B:** Well you can now use your controller to chop vegetables and slice food. You also use it to boil ingredients or grill them on the barbecue.
**A:** It works really well on the Wii, doesn't it? I thought the gameplay was excellent.
**B:** There were a few little problems, and the motion sensor didn't capture every movement perfectly, but yeah, in general, it works very well.
**A:** What was your favorite thing about the game?
**B:** The graphics are terrific. They are just fantastic on the Wii, and they're now in 3D, too.
**A:** I also thought that the character of Mama was hilarious. Some of the things she says are just crazy.
**B:** So what was your favorite recipe?
**A:** I absolutely loved making the chocolate chip cookies. In fact, I then used the recipe in real life and made a box of them for my friends.
**B:** My favorite was a disaster. I was making a hamburger, and it fell on the floor. Then Mama's dog ate it!
**A:** I remember that! That was pretty funny. So, who would you recommend this game for, Leila?
**B:** You can learn it very quickly, so I think it's fun for a party with your friends.
**A:** I agree. It's also great for kids because it's not violent like a shoot 'em up or something like that.
**B:** So thumbs up for Cooking Mama. Four stars from me.
**A:** Oh, I give it five.
**B:** Jake, you're so predictable!
**A:** What can I say? It was lots of fun.
**B:** OK, thanks everyone, and don't forget to tune into our next podcast on Saturday. Bye for now!

# Track Listing

| Transcript | Content | Track |
|---|---|---|
| Opening | | 1 |
| 1.1 | Page 3, Exercise 6 | 2 |
| 1.2 | Page 6, Listening, Exercises 1 & 2 | 3 |
| 2.1 | Page 12, Functional Language, Exercise 1 | 4 |
| 2.2 | Page 12, Listening, Exercises 1 & 2 | 5 |
| 3.1 | Page 15, Exercise 6 | 6 |
| 3.2 | Page 18, Listening, Exercises 1 & 2 | 7 |
| T1 | Page 21, Progress Test 1, Listening | 8 |
| 4.1 | Page 26, Listening, Exercises 1 & 2 | 9 |
| 5.1 | Page 29, Exercise 5 | 10 |
| 5.2 | Page 32, Listening, Exercise 1 | 11 |
| 6.1 | Page 35, Exercise 6 | 12 |
| 6.2 | Page 38, Listening, Exercises 1–3 | 13 |
| T2 | Page 41, Progress Test 2, Listening | 14 |

# IRREGULAR VERBS

| INFINITIVE | PAST SIMPLE | PAST PARTICIPLE |
|---|---|---|
| be | was, were | been |
| beat | beat | beaten |
| become | became | become |
| begin | began | begun |
| bend | bent | bent |
| bite | bit | bitten |
| bleed | bled | bled |
| blow | blew | blown |
| break | broke | broken |
| bring | brought | brought |
| build | built | built |
| buy | bought | bought |
| catch | caught | caught |
| choose | chose | chosen |
| come | came | come |
| cost | cost | cost |
| cut | cut | cut |
| do | did | done |
| dream | dreamed | dreamed |
| drink | drank | drunk |
| drive | drove | driven |
| eat | ate | eaten |
| fall | fell | fallen |
| feed | fed | fed |
| feel | felt | felt |
| fight | fought | fought |
| find | found | found |
| fly | flew | flown |
| forbid | forbade | forbidden |
| forget | forgot | forgotten |
| forgive | forgave | forgiven |
| freeze | froze | frozen |
| get | got | got |
| give | gave | given |
| go | went | gone, been |
| grow | grew | grown |
| have | had | had |
| hear | heard | heard |
| hide | hid | hidden |
| hold | held | held |
| keep | kept | kept |
| know | knew | known |
| learn | learned | learned |
| leave | left | left |
| lend | lent | lent |

| INFINITIVE | PAST SIMPLE | PAST PARTICIPLE |
|---|---|---|
| let | let | let |
| lie | lay | lain |
| lose | lost | lost |
| make | made | made |
| mean | meant | meant |
| meet | met | met |
| pay | paid | paid |
| put | put | put |
| read / rid / | read / rɛd / | read / rɛd / |
| ride | rode | ridden |
| ring | rang | rung |
| rise | rose | risen |
| run | ran | run |
| say | said | said |
| see | saw | seen |
| sell | sold | sold |
| send | sent | sent |
| set | set | set |
| shake | shook | shaken |
| shine | shone | shone |
| shoot | shot | shot |
| show | showed | shown |
| shut | shut | shut |
| sing | sang | sung |
| sit | sat | sat |
| sleep | slept | slept |
| smell | smelled | smelled |
| speak | spoke | spoken |
| spend | spent | spent |
| split | split | split |
| stand | stood | stood |
| steal | stole | stolen |
| stick | stuck | stuck |
| swim | swam | swum |
| take | took | taken |
| teach | taught | taught |
| tear | tore | torn |
| tell | told | told |
| think | thought | thought |
| throw | threw | thrown |
| understand | understood | understood |
| upset | upset | upset |
| wake | woke | woken |
| wear | wore | worn |
| win | won | won |
| write | wrote | written |